# REACHING
*for the*
# MOON

The Autobiography of NASA Mathematician
## KATHERINE JOHNSON

# REACHING
## *for the*
# MOON

*The Autobiography of NASA Mathematician*
# KATHERINE JOHNSON

Atheneum

**ATHENEUM BOOKS FOR YOUNG READERS**
New York London Toronto Sydney New Delhi

A
atheneum

ATHENEUM BOOKS FOR YOUNG READERS
An imprint of Simon & Schuster Children's Publishing Division
1230 Avenue of the Americas, New York, New York 10020
This work is a memoir. It reflects the author's present recollections of her experiences over a period of years.
Text copyright © 2019 by Katherine Johnson
Cover front panel (background) photographs copyright © 2019 by NASA
Cover front panel (foreground) photograph courtesy of Katherine Johnson
Chapter-opener art courtesy of Katherine Johnson and NASA
All rights reserved, including the right of reproduction in whole or in part in any form.
ATHENEUM BOOKS FOR YOUNG READERS is a registered trademark of Simon & Schuster, Inc. Atheneum logo is a trademark of Simon & Schuster, Inc.
For information about special discounts for bulk purchases, please contact Simon & Schuster Special Sales at 1-866-506-1949 or business@simonandschuster.com.
The Simon & Schuster Speakers Bureau can bring authors to your live event. For more information or to book an event, contact the Simon & Schuster Speakers Bureau at 1-866-248-3049 or visit our website at www.simonspeakers.com.
Also available in an Atheneum Books for Young Readers hardcover edition
Cover design by Greg Stadnyk
Interior design by Karyn Lee
The text for this book was set in Electra.
Manufactured in the United States of America
1020 OFF
First Atheneum Books for Young Readers paperback edition May 2020
2  4  6  8  10  9  7  5  3
The Library of Congress has cataloged the hardcover edition as follows:
Names: Johnson, Katherine G., author.
Title: Reaching for the Moon : the autobiography of NASA mathematician Katherine Johnson.
Description: First edition. | New York, New York : Atheneum Books for Young Readers, an imprint of Simon & Schuster Children's Publishing Division, [2019] | Audience: Ages 8–12. | Audience: Grades 4 to 6.
Identifiers: LCCN 2019003873| ISBN 9781534440838 (hc) | ISBN 9781534440845 (pbk) | ISBN 9781534440852 (eBook)
Subjects: LCSH: Johnson, Katherine G.—Juvenile literature. | United States. National Aeronautics and Space Administration—Officials and employees—Juvenile literature. | African American women mathematicians—Biography—Juvenile literature. | African American women—Biography—Juvenile literature. | Women mathematicians—Biography—Juvenile literature. | Apollo 11 (Spacecraft)
Classification: LCC QA29.J64 J64 2019 | DDC 510.92 [B]—dc23 LC record available at
https://lccn.loc.gov/2019003873

I'd like to dedicate this book to the memory of my father,
Joshua Coleman, and my mother, Joylette Lowe Coleman,
as well as to the children whom my story will inspire
to reach for the moon in their own lives.

# CHAPTER 1

It's not every day you wake up with a mission on your mind, but I had a mission and I was determined to accomplish it. Except for the sound of Mama humming and the clinking of dishes as she washed them in the sink, the house was quiet. Moments earlier Daddy had left for work and my brothers and sister had set off to school. As I sat at the kitchen table still fiddling with my oatmeal, I couldn't get my brother Charlie out of my mind. I kept revisiting the scene at the kitchen table the night before, when he'd struggled with his math homework.

First Mama had tried to assist him with it. Back before she'd had Horace, Margaret, Charlie, and me, she had been a teacher. She should have been able to help him figure out his schoolwork.

But the way he had slumped over onto one elbow had signaled that he was feeling frustrated.

"Sit up straight," Mama had told him, and he did.

Horace and Margaret were steadily scribbling away at their assignments, apparently unbothered by Charlie's challenges.

"Maybe you can explain it better than I can, Josh," Mama said to Daddy, who was sitting in the front room

My parents, Joshua and Joylette Coleman.

reading the *White Sulphur Sentinel*, our town's newspaper. Daddy loved to read the paper. He also read the almanac. Mama adored us, but she was very orderly and from time to time she could be a bit strict. Our father was a little more relaxed.

Daddy set the paper down and slowly unfurled

himself from his favorite chair. More than six feet tall, he towered above most everyone.

"Let's see what we can do here, Son," he said, sitting down and scooting closer to his youngest son, the chair scraping loudly across the oak floor.

Daddy put his left arm around Charlie, who leaned into him.

"I can't figure it out," Charlie said, his lack of confidence evident in his voice.

"Yes, you can," Daddy told him. "We just have to explain it so that you get it. Once you understand the background of any idea, you can figure any problem out for yourself."

Daddy's personality could be more comforting than Mama's. Numbers were also Daddy's strength. He may have had only a sixth-grade education, but he was really good with figures. Envisioning things was one of his strong points. He was so good that he could look at an entire oak, pine, or even a chestnut tree, and tell you how many logs it would yield once it had been cut down. We even lived in a home he had built for us.

Charlie was two years older than me, but for some

reason he seemed to be a little slow. At least, that's what I thought back then. I would be well into adulthood before I discovered that the issue wasn't that he was slow. The truth of the matter was that I was fast. It turned out that I was very gifted in math.

Math had always come easily to me. I loved numbers and numbers loved me. They followed me everywhere. No matter what I did, I was always finding something to count: the floorboards, the cracks in the sidewalk, the trees as I walked by, the train cars stacked with timber and those piled with coal that lumbered

Me at age two with my brothers and sister.

along the edge of our town each day. The number of times the train engineers blew the whistle as they traveled through the trees, echoing off the granite bedrock that rose above us and formed the valley within which our town, White Sulphur Springs, West Virginia, was nestled.

That was just the way that my mind worked. One, two, three, four, five, six, seven, eight forks. One, two, three, four, five, six, seven, eight plates. One, two, three serving spoons. Mama was very well organized, but my mind took her sense of order one step further. I always knew how many of everything there were. Things were there and could be counted and accounted for, so that's what I did.

So when Charlie found it hard to understand numbers, it really bothered me. And it disturbed me even more when he didn't understand even after both Mama and Daddy had tried to teach them to him.

At that point I decided to take things into my own hands. And that was why, even though I was only four years old, I told my plan to Mama, then walked out the front door, then four steps across the porch, eight steps down the front stairs, and five steps down the front walk, and set off toward the school.

As I marched out of our front yard and turned onto the sidewalk, I waved at Mrs. Hopkins, who was sweeping the front porch of her family's two-story house across our street. Church Street was the center of Colored life in White Sulphur Springs. Back then the same people we now call

African American or Black were called Colored or Negro. (It's important not to use those words to describe people today or you will certainly offend them.)

I strode slightly uphill past five houses and St. James United Methodist Church, where we worshipped, to the corner of Barton Road. That's where Church Street ended, as what had been a slight rise suddenly became very steep—too steep to sled after the snow fell. It was covered with maple, sycamore, and pine trees, and during the spring and summer months, grass.

About one hundred yards up that hill ran the Chesapeake and Ohio Railway tracks, where black and navy-blue trains with a yellow Cheshire cat painted on them rumbled through town twice daily, morning and evening. The C&O trains carried coal, lumber, and supplies as well as people from the Virginia coast (which was about six hours southeast) northwestward through the Allegheny Mountains, part of the Appalachian mountain range of West Virginia and southern Ohio. The C&O then carried its load over the Ohio River, across that state on into Detroit and other parts of Michigan. Some trains traveled even farther westward into Indiana and on to the growing industrial cities of Gary, Indiana, and Chicago, Illinois.

A passenger train also rolled through town, carrying not only travelers of modest means but also the well-appointed private coaches that the wealthy magnates of that era owned and used to travel around the country.

I turned left onto Barton and followed it one block until I came to a dirt path on my right. About one hundred feet up that path sat the Mary McLeod Bethune Grade School, the white wooden two-room schoolhouse where our town's Colored children were educated. The White children who lived in White Sulphur, as we affectionately called our town, went to the all-White school across town that the Colored students weren't allowed to attend.

The reason that Colored children and White children went to separate schools dated way back to slavery. Many White people convinced themselves that Colored people were an inferior race and so justified using guns, whippings, beatings, rape, and other violence to enslave Colored people and force them to work for Whites. These attitudes and behaviors were prevalent for many decades after slavery ended, including in education.

In its 1857 *Dred Scott* decision, our nation's highest court, the Supreme Court, ruled that Colored people were an "inferior and subordinate class of beings" as compared to Whites. Many White people then used the ruling to justify ongoing efforts to degrade and exploit Colored people. Then, in its 1896 *Plessy v. Ferguson* decision, the Supreme Court legalized "separate but equal" facilities that were segregated by race. But everyone knew that separate also meant unequal. And that is why Mary McLeod Bethune was a two-room school located on a dirt road rather than a paved one like the all-White schools.

Despite these considerable obstacles, Colored people fought for our rights and took pride in our achievements. We engaged in self-help, educated ourselves and one another, and fought against laws and racial violence set up to oppress us and keep us "in our place," as many White people described our inferior position in American society.

This brings me to Mary McLeod Bethune, a Colored woman born shortly after the end of slavery whose parents had been not only enslaved but also denied a formal education. The only one of her seventeen siblings able to obtain an education, she found knowledge to be so valuable that she shared what she was learning with everyone around her. She'd started teaching others back in the late 1800s. By the time I was born, on August 26, 1918, she was a famous educator and the founder of the Daytona Educational and Industrial Training School for Negro Girls (now Bethune-Cookman University), in Florida. She also helped lead the National Council of Negro Women, an organization focused on uplifting and improving the lives of Negroes by crusading for their rights to a quality education, the ability to vote, job opportunities, safety from racial violence, and more.

At the elementary school named in her honor, four grades were housed in each classroom. Mrs. Leftwich taught first through fourth grades in one room. That was the classroom that Charlie was in. Mr. Arter, the principal, taught fifth through seventh in the other, educating Horace and Margaret, whom I called Sister.

All totaled there were about twenty children in the first through fourth grades, and there was about the same number of older children. Now, far more Colored children than that lived in White Sulphur Springs, but many of them had to work to help their families have enough to eat. Though a high school existed to educate the White children, no school existed for Colored children after they finished the seventh grade.

I walked ninety-seven steps to the front door of the school, then used all my weight to open it wide enough to let myself in.

I then pulled up a chair next to Charlie, trying to be as quiet as possible.

"Why, what are you doing here, Katherine Coleman?" Mrs. Leftwich asked.

"I came to help my brother," I said.

"Aww, Katherine, that's sweet of you," she said. "But Charlie is two years older than you. You haven't even started school yet."

"Yes, ma'am," I said. "But I know how to help him."

"Okay, well, you just sit still and be quiet," she said.

"Yes, ma'am," I responded dutifully. I could tell she didn't believe me.

Yet while my brother worked on his math lesson, I whispered and helped him as quietly as I could. Mrs. Leftwich kept coming back to Charlie's seat and looking over our shoulders.

"You *are* helping him, aren't you?" she asked after standing there for a while.

"Yes, ma'am," I told her.

I'm not sure if she believed I was helping or if she was just trying to be nice to me. But Charlie and I figured out the answers together. When school was dismissed, I walked home with Charlie and the rest of the children and thought nothing of it.

One Saturday morning, I was helping Mama put dishes away when we heard one, two, three, four, five, six, seven, eight footsteps walking up the front stairs and onto the porch.

"Joylette, are you home?" a woman's voice called out to my mother by her first name as her knuckles rapped on the door.

"Who's there?" Mama answered as she finished drying a serving bowl and put down her dish towel.

"Rosa Leftwich," said the voice.

What was the schoolteacher doing at our house?

"Oh, hello!" my mother answered, ushering Mrs. Leftwich into our home. "It's good to see you. I hope that nothing's wrong."

"Oh, no, everything's fine," Mrs. Leftwich said.

"Good!" Mama said. "Well, Katherine and I were just drying dishes and straightening up. Why don't you come join us in the kitchen?"

Mama pulled out a seat at the kitchen table. Mrs. Leftwich sat, and my mother poured her a cup of coffee and offered her some homemade applesauce.

"Katherine picked all the apples herself," Mama informed her.

Well, after Mama had picked me up so I could reach them.

Mrs. Leftwich and Mama exchanged pleasantries, and I entertained myself counting and recounting the silverware.

"Well, I'm not sure if you are aware," Mrs. Leftwich began, "but K-a-t-h-e-r-i-n-e came to the s-c-h-o-o-l last week."

My mother mouthed something to Mrs. Leftwich and

motioned to me. Perhaps Mrs. Leftwich had forgotten that I was in the room.

"The person tried to h-e-l-p C-h-a-r-l-i-e with his m-a-t-h."

My mother pointed toward me.

Mrs. Leftwich looked at me and smiled.

I may have been only four, but I could understand everything she was saying. By then I could spell lots of words and already knew my multiplication tables.

Mama had been teaching me new words all the time. Between her training as a teacher and Daddy's natural knack for numbers, education was highly valued in our home.

So I looked at Mama, and Mama looked at me. She shrugged.

"You don't have to spell those words," I told Mrs. Leftwich. "I know what you're saying; I already know how to spell."

Mrs. Leftwich's eyes widened.

"You know how to spell?" she asked, looking at my mother in disbelief.

"Yes, ma'am," I told her.

"So, do you understand what I was saying?"

"Yes, ma'am."

"What was I saying?"

"That I came to school and helped Charlie with math."

"Well, I'll be!" She gasped. "Who taught you how to spell?"

"Mama and Sister," I answered.

"You're serious!" Mrs. Leftwich exclaimed.

"Yes, ma'am. Mama teaches me spelling every night."

Shocked, Mrs. Leftwich looked at my mother.

"We spell and we read and we learn math, don't we, Katherine?" Mama said.

"Well, if you can already spell, Katherine, you need to be in school," Mrs. Leftwich said.

"Yes, ma'am. That's why I came to help Charlie. Sometimes he's slow."

"Katherine, how would you like it if I got some other children together and we start a kindergarten class?"

"I'd like to go to kindergarten," I said. Being very inquisitive, no matter where I was, I always wanted to know what was going on. It was also important for me to understand why things were the way they were.

Apparently, after she left, Mrs. Leftwich talked to some other parents. After that she started working with a handful of children. That summer she started a kindergarten class in her home. Now, rather than being left with Mama at home, I went to class at Mrs. Leftwich's.

When school began that fall, I started in the second grade. Suddenly I was a year ahead of Charlie and two years behind Sister, who was the smartest of all of us—even smarter than Horace, who was older than her. But Sister had a wayward eye—it didn't look straight. By then I could already tell that people often underestimated her.

A few years after that they skipped me over fifth grade as well.

Horace and Sister remained ahead of me in school.

At first the other kids and their parents seemed to make a big deal about the fact that I'd been skipped forward in class. Everyone fussed over me at church. But then everyone got used to my being there and I went back to being Katherine.

I loved to learn so much that going to school alone wasn't enough. I would go to the library as well. I loved to read, but the librarians allowed me to take out only one book at a time, though I could have read more than that.

Most days I would walk back home from school with the other kids. We would explore the forest, climb trees, or play jacks and kickball. When the first snow fell, we would sled down the hill behind our house, doing our best to avoid the apple tree at the bottom. Then I would go inside, thaw off, and help Mama put dinner on the table. After dinner we would work on our homework.

During the week, Mama would spend much of her day cooking. Back then, before you could buy prepared foods or go through the drive-through, it took a considerable part of the day to create three full-course meals from scratch, morning, noon, and night.

Mama kept chickens, which Daddy accused her of spoiling. Because when the time would come to eat one for dinner, she wouldn't have the heart to kill it. So one of the boys would chase the chicken she wanted, catch it, and wring its neck—break it. Wringing a chicken's neck doesn't kill it right away, so she would put a big tub on top of it. Then we'd listen to the chicken running around like crazy under the tub until it died and the noise stopped—

something we no longer do today because it's inhumane, but back then it was just how we fed ourselves. At that point Mama would pick the chicken up and drop it into boiling water, which would loosen the feathers so that she could pull them off. Once the chicken had been plucked, she'd bake or fry it for dinner. In addition to fresh vegetables, our dinners often consisted of chicken or meat loaf, beans, potatoes, and gravy. We would buy milk, bacon, and bread from the grocery store. Often I'd be the one my parents would send on that errand.

Mama also spent time washing and ironing. She did our family's laundry, but also that of some White families, as many other Colored women did to make ends meet. The laundry Mama took in included that of a White Episcopal priest, Reverend Eder, the priest in charge at St. Thomas Episcopal Church. Back then most people didn't have washing machines, so Mama washed clothes by hand in a big green tub. She rubbed clothes against a washboard with a surface of corrugated metal to help get the dirt out. After she was finished washing, she attached porcelain rollers to the tub. She would then feed the clothes into the rollers and turn the crank to squeeze the excess water out so that she could hang the clothes on the line to dry.

Mama also could sew. She sewed our dresses. We didn't have more than we needed, and everything we owned was practical. Back then flour came in big sacks. She would often make our dresses out of flour sacks.

On Sundays we attended St. James, where our family sat in the second row to the right. Daddy taught Sunday school, and I would help him. After church we'd come home for dinner. Sister would set the table, and afterward I'd help wash and dry the dishes. Then we'd go back for evening service.

Only one time, when we got a little older, did Daddy let us sit in the back of the church with the rest of the children our age. But during service, one of the other kids acted out and there was a small commotion. Though we weren't involved, it got Daddy's attention. He stood up, turned around, and looked at us.

"All of mine," he said.

We knew what that meant, so we got up and moved to the front of the church. That's just how Daddy was.

Dinnertime was important for our family, especially on Sundays, when the preacher and his wife often came over.

Daddy would bless our food, and then we would talk about our day as we sat at the table. Often that conversation included indirectly discussing racism. We would wonder aloud about things like why we couldn't go the ice rink with the White children or why we had to sit in the balcony of the movie theater. There was no way to explain segregation's daily humiliations and inequality, so there wasn't much discussion about the reasons. You just had to know the rules, know your place, and stay in it. Doing that increased the odds that you would be safe and unharmed.

"You are no better than anyone else, but nobody else is better than you," Daddy would emphasize to us over and over, even as he guided us to understand the restrictions of segregation.

Once dinner was over, we would clear the kitchen table and homework would begin. On Friday nights, for entertainment, we would often help Mama bake a cake or we would test our minds by working puzzles or playing checkers and other table games.

* * * * * * * * * * * * * *

We hadn't always lived in White Sulphur Springs. Until I was two, we resided in the country. Now that I look back upon it, it was country life that formed my family's values and are instilled in me to this day.

Before we'd moved into town, Daddy had owned a very large farm and log-cabin farmhouse called Dutch Run located out on Big Draft Road in Oakhurst, a small rural community about three miles outside of town.

Now, how a Colored man back in that time came to own so much land and a house, I'm not quite sure, especially when he lacked much formal education. Some people say that he was the descendant of Colored people who had never been enslaved and as a result had been able to accumulate more than the average Colored person. Others say that one of his grandfathers was a White army colonel and one of his grandmothers was an enslaved Colored woman whom the colonel had forced himself on. As the story goes, the colonel subsequently provided for her and their mixed-race children. Perhaps some land from that union might have been handed down. It's not hard to imagine that some sort of privilege may have been extended to him.

Looking back on things now, it is clear that as a very fair-skinned Negro, my daddy enjoyed some advantages that darker-skinned people didn't. As his children, we were on the fair-skinned side as well. Back then people believed that one drop of Black blood tainted the "superior race," but having White blood made you "better."

Regardless, we lived at Dutch Run until I became a toddler. At that point he sold the farm. Then he moved us into 30 Church Street, the house he had built for us in town, which would make it easier for us to attend school.

Though we don't know exactly how it happened, some White man must have purchased the land in town for Daddy; I don't know who, how, or why. I do know that Colored people weren't allowed to buy land back then.

What Daddy lacked in formal education, he made up for with his profound knowledge of and appreciation for the natural world. Until we'd moved into town, Daddy had been a farmer. He and Mama were very independent on the farm, raising just about everything our family needed to eat:

beans, greens, peas, potatoes, corn, wheat, apples, grapes. We also had chickens and pigs.

Back then the only things Mama purchased from the store were coffee beans, granulated sugar, salt, and pepper. During the fall she would spend much of her day canning enough food to feed us over the winter.

Though farm life offered my parents a measure of independence that life in town didn't, it was difficult then, and it remains difficult today. Farmers are dependent upon factors such as whether the sun shines enough or too much, when the rain comes and how much falls, and whether pests like the apple moth will undermine their crops and leave them with little to harvest, or whether frost or an early snowfall will leave them with scarcely anything to show for their months of work.

In the Allegheny Mountains it was essential to be able to feed your family, especially during the winters. That's when the roads became treacherous and often impassable with snow and ice. Having canned enough food to feed yourself could mean the difference between surviving until spring or starving. This was where the laws of segregation would sometimes bow down to the laws of survival.

As a practical matter, even though the White people of West Virginia required Colored people to live in separate neighborhoods, out in Oakhurst that luxury didn't always exist.

Plus, no one family could afford all of the different equipment—the plows, the threshing machines, the corn shellers, and so on—that they needed to farm all their land. So each family would buy one big piece of equipment, and they would all share it, regardless of race. That way everyone wasn't investing in duplicate equipment or machines that would sit idle until the same time next year. Come harvest time, the entire community would gather together and work in one another's fields—the White families as well as Colored families cooperating to ensure that everyone survived.

Women and men often took on gender roles that were more traditional and distinct than their roles are today. The men typically worked in the fields, while women would manage the family's garden and kitchen. Cultivating a large garden, too, was difficult work—stooping over long rows of peas or collard greens, or keeping the rabbits or deer from eating your food. It often took all day to create every meal from scratch, laboring in a hot kitchen to cook enough sustenance to support dawn-to-dusk physical labor.

It wasn't unusual during harvest season for women to prepare breakfast and dinner at home, then come together to serve the midday meal, everyone gathering in one house to eat—typically the house of the family whose fields were being worked. In this way everyone was well fed and could get back to work more quickly than if each person walked or rode his horse home to eat and then came back after lunch. Saving precious daylight hours could mean the difference between harvesting the food before the first frost or not, and having enough nourishment for the winter or not.

Since survival was a practical matter, some of the rules of segregation that were strictly enforced in other locations didn't exist to the same extent in Oakhurst. Though racial segregation was imposed in town, during planting season and the harvest, Colored people and Whites became just a community of farmers coming together to help one another live. Though country children attended segregated schools during the daytime, after school we played together.

The belief that people should convene to help one another was valued in my family. You always lent a hand to other human beings. Perhaps that's also how I learned from an early age to not always adhere to the customs of the color line.

When Daddy wasn't farming, he was often cutting trees. There were lots of big trees all around the family farm and the region, where during the summer everything turned emerald green. In fact, the Meadow River Lumber Company operated the world's largest sawmill not too far away, along the Meadow River between the Sewell and Simms Mountains, at the western edge of Greenbrier County.

Cutting down a tree may look easy, but it's really hard. You have to know things like whether the tree is solid or whether any of it is rotten in the middle, the type of wood you're cutting, and the angle at which you want to make it fall. You cut a Norway maple differently from a sycamore maple. If you don't calculate that right, the tree can fall onto your house—or onto your head and kill you. Even today, logging is very dangerous work.

Daddy and his crew would cut trees down, then use his horse-drawn wagon to haul lumber from the logging camps to the mill for cutting. Daddy owned workhorses and show horses. His workhorses hauled timber around. His show horses, who were named Bill and Frank, transported our family in a horse-drawn buggy. He would also use the buggy to carry White people around, a way of making additional money.

We lived in horse country, and Daddy was a horse man. He loved horses, and somehow horses knew that they could trust him. White people would bring him their horses and he would tell them what was wrong. A horse whisperer was what they called him. Daddy was like a veterinarian without a formal degree. He could calm horses down and make animals well. Daddy would wake up in the middle of the night because somehow while he was sleeping he would hear a heifer—a cow—moaning because she was in labor.

"That animal is in trouble." He'd know based on the sound of her cries.

He would get out of bed and go help the heifer deliver her baby.

Daddy also had common sense. He'd look at the color of the sky at sunset and know what weather lay on the horizon: "Red sky at night, sailors' delight; red sky in the morning, sailors take warning." On weekends, he and I would often head back out to the country, going on long walks along dirt paths, across grassy knolls, and over the forest floor carpeted with leaves, gold and brown. We would ramble through the hills, searching for wild blackberries and huckleberries so Mama could bake a pie. Daddy would point out the moths, carpenter ants, and roly-poly bugs beneath the bark of dead logs. I would help him pick out flat rocks to skip atop the chilly water cascading down the creek.

On one particular journey, when I was four, we stopped for a moment to catch our breath.

"What's this warm thing I'm standing on?" I asked, sensing something unusual beneath my bare feet.

Daddy bent over to look.

"Be still. Don't move!" he said, standing quickly as he reached over his shoulder and pulled out his rifle—all in one smooth movement.

*BAM!*

I jumped, and a spray of leaves and dirt flew up into the air. Then Daddy kicked at something with his boot.

"That was a snake, a copperhead," he told me as he

picked up what was left of the snake with a stick. "Watch out for copperheads, Katherine; they're poisonous."

I inched closer to the stick. The snake's body was draped over it.

"You can always tell a copperhead by its markings," Daddy told me. "Do you see that hourglass marking that's skinny in the middle and wider on its sides?"

"Yes," I said.

"That's how you can tell them."

I always felt so safe whenever Daddy was near.

Though life on the farm had been simple and carefree, in town the lines between the races were much clearer. While Main Street was the downtown for the entire city, parts of White Sulphur were distinctly Colored.

Daddy had built our new home, called the Big House, in the main Colored part of town. The Big House in White Sulphur was better than Dutch Run. There were four rooms on the ground floor and a main stairway to the second floor. Upstairs there were four bedrooms: one for our mother and father, one for the boys, one for us girls, and an extra one.

The bathroom was upstairs on the second floor. That house was large by anyone's standards.

Wide porches—one upstairs and one downstairs—ran the expanse of the front of the house. The ceiling of each was painted sky blue. Sitting there, you would see Colored life in White Sulphur pass by. I loved to relax on the porch with my father.

Our house on Church Street.

"Good morning, Mr. Coleman," people would say as they walked by.

"Good morning," my father would reply.

One of the best things about our house was that it was the first on the block to have indoor plumbing; everyone else used the bathroom in their outhouse, a shack with a hole in the ground and a seat you would sit on as you relieved yourself. We also had the first telephone on Church Street. Our phone number was 228. It was a party line, which meant you shared your line with other people. The calls came in to a central operator sitting at a switchboard at the phone company downtown. The operator would pick up the phone and manually route the call to your house. If somebody else was on the line, you had to wait. If it was an emergency, you could ask the other person to hang up. But people didn't stay on the phone forever, as they do today.

Church Street was about two city blocks long by today's standards.

We had one White neighbor, who lived on the far end on our side. We didn't really know him. The White people in White Sulphur didn't bother you, but they didn't mix with you either.

Walking from that end up in the direction of our house, you'd pass two homes before you got to that of Mr. Arter. Then you'd pass First Baptist and Haywood's, the only restaurant in town where Colored people could eat. You'd walk by four more houses before you got to our house. Four houses beyond us you'd run into St. James, where Church Street dead-ended at Barton. Crump Barbershop, where Daddy got his hair cut, was across the street from Haywood's. Daddy's mother lived in a little one-story house next door to Crump's. Daddy kept a beautiful garden in her backyard, with rows of string beans, rhubarb, potatoes, onions, scallions, carrots, radishes, and beans. We ate from that garden during much of the year.

The Baptist and Methodist churches were the only ones that Colored people in White Sulphur could attend. Back then, each had a part-time preacher who would deliver service on two Sundays a month. The Methodist preacher preached on the first and third Sunday, the Baptist preacher on the second and fourth. Since most everyone went to church every week, that meant the Methodists attended the Baptist church and the Baptists attended the Methodist church on the weeks when their pastor wasn't preaching. During the summer they held a combined picnic. They also combined their vacation Bible school, where children learned about the Bible during summer vacation.

St. Thomas Episcopal Church, where Reverend Eder presided, was on Main Street in the center of town. But only White people could attend. There was only one God, but segregation meant that White people and Colored people couldn't worship Him in the same place. We let God be the judge of that.

Though people lived there all year long, White Sulphur Springs was a vacation town. Known as the "Queen of the Watering Places" in the South, it was where the well-heeled vacationers from Virginia's coast and other Southern locations would escape summer's heat and humidity. Because it was located two thousand feet high in the mountains, White Sulphur's climate was much more comfortable than other southerly regions were.

Our town got its name from a freshwater mineral

bath that bubbled up from deep underground. Before the European settlers arrived and killed off most of the indigenous people, Greenbrier County was part of the Can-tuc-kee territory, where the Shawnee and Cherokee peoples lived. According to legend, a young Shawnee couple slipped away to spend time alone. Their chief caught them together unsupervised, became angry, and shot two arrows toward them. The first killed the boy; the second whistled past the girl, pierced the ground, and supposedly created the springs. After the last drop of spring water has been drunk, the young woman's suitor is supposed to return to life.

That's the story according to legend. Scientifically, a thermal spring comes from geothermally heated groundwater rising from the Earth's crust.

Regardless of the water's source, for centuries people believed that it cured rheumatism's stiff joints, as well as skin problems, respiratory illnesses, menstrual cramps, fevers, and so on. Folks would travel from across the South and beyond in order to visit the spring. Our town was also known for the Battle of White Sulphur Springs, a bloody conflict fought during the Civil War, where almost four hundred Union and Confederate soldiers were lost.

During the mid-1800s, an impressive six-story, snow-colored resort called the Greenbrier Hotel was built at the springs. Indeed, the Greenbrier looked so much like the White House that it was once known as "Old White." Before the Civil War, five sitting presidents vacationed there, as did judges, lawyers, diplomats, slaveholders, and merchants—mostly from Southern states. Only two years before I was born, in 1916, President and Mrs. Woodrow Wilson spent Easter at the Greenbrier. The grandparents of President John F. Kennedy, who wasn't yet born, honeymooned there when I was two months old.

During the years right after my birth and well into the Roaring Twenties, the Greenbrier was very popular among the industrialists and other extremely wealthy people in American society. The C&O Railway owned the two-hundred-and-fifty-room property and delivered its guests—who, depending on the season, would vacation in places like the Greenbrier; Newport, Rhode Island; and Palm Beach, Florida—in their private coaches right to the resort's front door. Indeed, the railroad stop was located right across Main Street from the resort. Passengers would step off the train and into a horse and carriage to be ridden across the road, their feet not even touching the ground. We towns-folk would gaze longingly at the visitors dressed so formally. The women would be attired in colorful ball gowns—blush pink, scarlet, sapphire blue, and forest green—and the men in tuxedos. From the outside, they seemed to live a wonder-ful life. The rest of us had to travel by foot, saddle up a horse, or maybe ride a horse and buggy to get around.

Daddy moved us into the town that developed around the Greenbrier, to make it easy for us to go to school. His sixth-grade education was not unusual. He had been born at a time when education was a luxury for Colored people, particularly in rural areas. Because they were often denied the opportunity to receive schooling around the turn of the twentieth century, when Daddy was born, about half of Colored people at that time were unable to read.

Because his own education had been prohibited, his children's was extremely important to him. If there was one thing Daddy would say, it was that he didn't want to raise any "dumb, ignorant children." He was determined that his children would go to college.

The wealthy guests of the Greenbrier created many sources of income for everyone, regardless of race. Whether at the Virginia Electric Company, the bank, or the Episcopal church, all of which Daddy now cleaned, in town there was work. He also took care of several rich people's summer homes during the fall and winter when they relocated to warmer places. They trusted my father with the keys to their homes, and he took care of everything during winter months when the homes were uninhabited. His honorable reputation preceded him, and his word was his bond—you could always trust what he said. Come spring, he would prepare the houses for the families to return during vacation season. He also drove rich people around with his show horses and buggy, which were way prettier than those at the Greenbrier.

Colored people were allowed to work at the Greenbrier, but they weren't permitted to stay there as guests. Colored women served as maids, babysitters, servers, and seamstresses. They unpacked trunks and pressed people's clothes. Colored men labored as bellmen and servers and busboys and porters, which were some of the best jobs they were able to obtain during those times. This type of work was also among the least hazardous—far safer and cleaner than what could be found in the coal mines, one of the area's major employers that offered some of the most dangerous jobs in the world. Daddy worked at the Greenbriar as a bellman in addition to doing side jobs.

I would go everywhere with Daddy. I especially loved accompanying him to his cleaning or handyman work or as he ran his errands downtown, where the White people worked.

"Good morning, Mrs. Burr," he would say to one of the White ladies with a tip of the hat, his cleaning bucket hanging from his free arm. Mrs. Burr's husband owned the Esso, the only gas station in town.

"Good morning, Josh," Mrs. Burr and other White women would reply, calling him by his first name.

Daddy was well respected; however, segregation had its rules, laws, and conventions. Although Colored people addressed Daddy as "mister," White people, including children, called him by his first name.

Even though Greenbrier's jobs were good for that era, Daddy didn't want his children to have to work there when they grew up, experiencing either its snubs or the perilous accusations that White people could capriciously make against Colored people—you never knew when.

Like many other Colored people of that era, he saw education as the pathway his children could follow to escape indignities and dangers, large and small. So for two years he sent Margaret away to continue her education. Then Daddy and Mama decided to take a leap of faith.

# CHAPTER 2

Nineteen twenty-six was the year that everything changed for the Coleman children, especially for me. Determined that all their children would receive the education they deserved, Daddy and Mama decided to leave the love and support of their family and community in White Sulphur and uproot us to Institute, West Virginia, home of the West Virginia Colored Institute.

Built in 1891, the West Virginia Colored Institute provided hope to many of our state's Negro citizens as we fought to obtain an education. For the first twenty years of its existence, the Institute offered a high school education and training in various vocations, such as agriculture. It also prepared teachers. By 1926, the school was on the verge of being able to offer diplomas in the liberal arts. Shortly thereafter it would be called West Virginia State College and begin granting four-year degrees.

During slavery, it had been illegal for enslaved people to read or write, and Whites killed many Colored people just for attempting to learn. In 1863, President Lincoln issued the Emancipation Proclamation, freeing enslaved people in the states that had rebelled. In the decades that followed, Colored people strove to educate themselves—organizing, creating self-help groups, running for office, fighting to change laws, founding schools, and so on. Their goal was to experience the joy and empowerment that education creates and to participate fully in American society.

The vast majority of White Southerners opposed education for Colored people, and even though Colored people paid taxes, governments refused to fund Colored schools. In fact, being an educator could be a very dangerous career. White supremacist groups like the Ku Klux Klan had a history of publicly hanging, or lynching, Colored teachers and burning down schools, homes, and churches. The

Klan would march and hold rallies to intimidate Colored people, its members' identities hidden beneath white sheets and pointed white hoods used to cover their faces. Mobs of the KKK's "night riders" on horseback bearing torches might appear in the yard of a Colored family after nightfall, threatening to burn down their home with them in it. Klan members would also ignite crosses in public locations, which was their signature way to strike terror into Colored people's hearts. Because Klan members concealed themselves, Colored people never felt safe, since they never truly knew which White people in their community were the KKK members and which ones knew who were in the Klan but wouldn't tell.

Before she'd had children, Mama had become a teacher out of her sense of mission and possibility. My parents felt hopeful that their children's futures would be better than their own. Daddy wanted his sons' existence to be easier than his own life of hard labor. He dreamed that maybe one day Colored people would be able to vacation at places like the Greenbrier right alongside the White people, rather than merely serving them.

So, fighting for their children's future, that September of 1926, Mama and Daddy decided to pack up the Big House and hire a man with a truck to drive us to Institute. We all piled in and for eight hours snaked our way along the Midland Trail through the steep emerald-green slopes of the Allegheny Mountains—past Ravenseye, past Lookout, past Chimney Corner and Kanawha Falls—the truck's flatbed piled high with our belongings. We ate the meals that Mama had packed for us, and relieved ourselves discreetly in the woods, unable to use the public rest areas, which were marked WHITES ONLY.

Once we arrived in Institute, Daddy took us to the home of Mama's cousin Nannie and her husband, who could rent us a house. The next step was for Daddy to look for employment.

Daddy woke up very early the next morning, dead set on accomplishing an important mission—getting work. Exhausted from packing up our house, loading it onto the truck, and unloading it again once we'd reached Institute, Daddy tarried at the kitchen table longer than usual, talking to Mama and peering into his cup of coffee.

At about eight a.m., he kissed me on my forehead and left, determinedly setting off on a walk across town and along the Institute's grassy campus, past both the livestock and the gardens that students helped to maintain.

Sometimes I reflect upon that day and consider what might have been on his mind. It would have been a familiar walk, since he'd brought Margaret to Institute to attend school over the previous years. Along his walk, I imagine he thought about all of the work it must have taken to build the beautiful redbrick buildings. It is likely the buildings had wooden frames. He would have begun calculating how many trees it had taken to build them.

The president's office of the West Virginia Colored Institute was located in room 101 of the Administration Building, known as Building A, a three-story-tall redbrick building with a five-story clock tower and a roof made of the bluestone shingles native to the area. The Institute's president, Dr. John W. Davis, was a graduate of Morehouse College. Founded in 1867, Morehouse's mission was to educate Black men for careers in ministry and teaching.

I presume that when Daddy reached the front doorway, he stopped, removed his hat, said a short prayer, and
admired the large wooden entryway. Knowing him, he
would have wondered how many doors had been cut from
that tree. Once he pushed the portal open, he walked up
three marble steps and through one of three arches. He
found himself in a grandiose lobby with white marble floors,
ceilings almost two stories high, and pendant lights hanging
from the ceiling. It wasn't as grandiose as the lobby of the
Greenbrier, yet it was grand and stately like a courthouse.

Daddy would have stood for a moment, taking in all the
details and admiring the bookish young men and women
scurrying past on their way to class. In addition to the administrative offices, Building A was home to the library, the
auditorium, and most of the classrooms. A young man ran
through the lobby, late to class, and bumped into Daddy.

"Excuse me, sir!" he said.

"No problem, young man," my father replied.

A lot was riding upon this meeting. Daddy felt nervous.

"May I help you, sir?" a smartly dressed, caramel-colored
woman inquired from behind a desk to his left.

My daddy, Joshua Coleman.

"Yes, ma'am," Daddy said, walking toward her, holding his hat in his hand, the floor gently creaking as he walked. "I am looking for the office of President John W. Davis."

"His office is right here, sir," the woman said, looking over the top of her reading glasses and inspecting Daddy's medium-gray three-button blazer and matching vest, charcoal-colored tie, and brown leather church shoes. "Do you have an appointment?"

"No, ma'am, I don't," Daddy replied. "My name is Joshua Coleman. My daughter attends school here, and my other children will begin this fall."

"Oh, you're Margaret Coleman's father," she said, her face softening and becoming pleasant.

"Yes, and my other children will begin this fall," he said.

"What a wonderful young woman she is," she said.

"Why, thank you," Daddy said. "I moved my entire family here and am looking for work. I was just hoping that President Davis would be able to give me a moment of his time."

"One minute, please," she said. Then she rapped gently on the door before entering.

Daddy fidgeted as he waited. Sending Margaret away to school had been challenging, emotionally and financially. He didn't have the money to send all of his children away to attend high school and college. Maintaining two residences would be too much for almost any man to handle, no matter his color. With all of his children enrolled in the school, Daddy hoped he might find work there.

The woman emerged and held the door open.

"President Davis will see you," she said pleasantly.

"Why, thank you, miss."

Slowly Daddy adjusted his jacket, took a deep breath, and followed the woman into President Davis's office.

"Good morning, Mr. Coleman," President Davis said, reaching out his hand.

"Good day, President Davis," Daddy said, gripping the president's hand and giving it a vigorous shake.

"Sit down," President Davis said. "Make yourself comfortable."

A fair-skinned man, President Davis was barely a shade darker than Daddy, but was considerably shorter. Daddy sat in front of his desk and placed his hat in his lap.

"This is a mighty impressive office you have here, sir," Daddy said, looking around the room as President Davis settled in behind his desk.

"Why, thank you. It suits me well," President Davis replied. "What can I do for you, sir?"

"Well, President Davis, yesterday I moved my family cross-state from White Sulphur Springs, over by the Virginia line, so that the rest of my children can attend the Institute. My daughter Margaret already goes here."

"I see," President Davis replied, attentively leaning forward across the desk.

"But I have four children to educate and a wife to care

for," Daddy continued. "I was wondering if you might have some work here at the Institute. I can clean. I can build and fix things. I can fell a tree. I can farm. I'm a horseman. . . ."

"Your vision for your family is commendable," President Davis said. "Unfortunately, Mr. Coleman, we don't have any positions available at this time." He sat back in his chair. "Perhaps you could check with me again early next year. What did you say your children's names were again?"

"Horace, Margaret, Charlie, and Katherine—they're all very smart."

"I'm sure they are, and they're very fortunate to have a father as determined as you are," President Davis said.

"Do you know of any work for a Colored man here in town?"

"I'm sorry, Mr. Coleman. I'm not sure that I do. I regret that I'm not able to be much help."

With that, Daddy shook President Davis's hand, thanked him for his time, and slowly walked home. Knowing how important this was to Daddy, I imagine he probably blinked back a few tears along the way. It wasn't easy for a Colored man to obtain work back then. After several additional days of searching unsuccessfully, Daddy returned the 122 miles to White Sulphur Springs by himself. There he labored long hours and extra jobs alone, without the love and companionship of his wife and children, as he sacrificed his own enjoyment and comfort so that we could be educated. For the next eight years we would live apart from Daddy whenever school was in session, and would travel back and forth between White Sulphur and Institute over holidays and summers until all four of us had completed both high school and four-year college programs.

I missed Daddy terribly. Since we didn't have a telephone, I wrote him a letter every day.

Living apart from Daddy required all hands on deck. Mama now took care of everything—grocery shopping, cooking, cleaning, washing our clothes, paying bills and tuition. She took in ironing for White people, which she did from home. Horace and Charlie got jobs too—cutting grass, delivering fresh milk to people's front doors, performing chores for the neighbors, doing odd jobs around campus, and delivering newspapers. Sister often helped Mama with her ironing work and tended to the house. Just nine years old, I was too young to work; my job was to make all the beds. It wasn't a hard life, but no one was standing around idle. Everyone did whatever had to be done.

I attended the primary school on the Institute's campus. Before long I was finishing my work early and helping my classmates with their studies. I loved helping other people, and after they adjusted to the fact that I was so much younger, they always accepted my support.

My siblings and I would walk home for lunch or take it with us in a brown paper bag. Our food was modest: bread and jelly.

Mama went to school a lot to check on our progress. As a former teacher, she knew where we were supposed to be in all of our classes. That's when she noticed that I had free time. I was extremely curious, just a busybody. Back then people believed that an idle mind was the devil's workshop — if you didn't stay busy, you would get into trouble.

Mama would try to keep me occupied reading books, helping around the house, learning how to sew and cook, and practicing the piano — typical girls' activities back then. Our schoolteachers taught us how to play piano. Both Sister and I were taught how to play church hymns. I learned how to make a simple skirt as well as to bake peach and cherry cobblers, crisscrossing the dough decoratively across the top.

I was extremely close with Horace and Charlie and loved to play with them. In fact, we were so close that I would rather be with them than almost anyone else. I became what we used to call a tomboy—a girl who engaged in activities that were traditionally associated with males. For instance, I learned how to play tennis; I was athletic. Several years later the boys would teach me how to ride a motorbike and drive a car, which few women did back then.

With Margaret and my brothers attending the Institute's high school, it wasn't unusual for me to wander across campus to see them. In fact, it was all Mama could do to keep up with me. Even back then I asked questions that most people didn't ask, and stepped over the unspoken lines that most girls and Colored people dared not cross.

My father's teaching had been instilled inside me: "You are no better than anyone else, but nobody else is better than you."

\* \* \* \* \* \* \* \* \* \* \* \*

I started high school the next year at just ten years old. By then most everybody knew Horace, Margaret, or Charlie—and if everybody knew them, that meant everybody knew me. At first everyone fussed again because I was so young. Before long I just blended in.

After class I played with President Davis's daughters, nicknamed Dit, Dot, and Dash—the same as the Morse code signals the military used to communicate—because they were such busybodies. Dit, whose real name was Constance, and I became best friends.

Here I am (center) at my eighth-grade graduation.

But the fact that I was attending high school posed quite a challenge for my mother, since suddenly my classmates were all teenagers. And though I found my classes interesting, I continued to learn more quickly than the other children. I was always tutoring and looking for new challenges. One man working in the school's business office had told me he'd give me five cents for every A that I earned.

"You're making me broke," he used to tell me. I took pride in acing my classes, plus our family needed every extra cent.

One day Mama walked me over to campus to talk to Professor James C. Evans, the head of the math department.

"Professor, Katherine finishes her lessons early," Mama said. "She has too much free time on her hands. Will you give her something to do? I don't care what it is. I just need to keep her busy, even if it means licking stamps!"

So Professor Evans gave me some administrative work to do. In the process he discovered that I didn't know how to type. That June, right when our family packed up all our belongings and Daddy picked us up and we headed back to White Sulphur, Professor Evans generously gave me his typewriter, a pack of paper, and the typing book to take home over the summer.

"When you get back in September, I want you to be able to type," he said. (And when classes resumed that fall, I could!)

Little did I know that moment would prove pivotal in my professional career.

It was always great to come home for the summers so that we could reconnect with Daddy, and for our family to be together again.

As each of the Coleman children became old enough, one by one we would work at the Greenbrier to save money for tuition and to cover the expense of living both in Institute and at the Big House. Most of the jobs for Colored people could be found at the Greenbrier or in related work. Because most of the lodging in White Sulphur Springs was Whites-only, the Colored people who had larger homes would often take in a chauffeur or a Pullman porter as a roomer. People particularly enjoyed taking in the Pullman porters, the Black men whom industrialist George Pullman hired to serve the sleeper cars on his trains. Not only would the porters regale them with tales of their travels and the lives of the super wealthy, but the porters often brought delicacies—unfamiliar foods, mixed nuts, and cakes from the train or beyond—which

Our family at our house on Church Street.

they would exchange for a discount on their room or the meals that the family prepared for them.

This was the Roaring Twenties, a time of great affluence and extravagance among wealthy Whites. The hotel was upgraded, doubling the number of rooms to five hundred and creating grand new facades and a new main entrance. In a town where many buildings were two stories at most, the Greenbrier's six stories seemed towering. Its eight columns stretching three stories high made the building look like a cross between the White House and a Southern plantation home. I counted 146 windows across the face of the building alone.

After disembarking at the train station across the street, guests would step into a horse-drawn carriage and be ridden to the three archways, each with a gaslight glowing between it and the next arch, at the hotel's entrance. At night the lights flickered with a warm and welcoming glow of gold. Holding on to wrought-iron balustrades, guests would then ascend thirty stairs that curved upward to the first-floor landing, whose sky-blue ceiling that Daddy had replicated at our house was like the heavens. They would then enter the hotel's grand lobby.

Inside the hotel was Greenbrier Avenue, with its black and white floor tiles forming a checkerboard, as well as columns and a center sitting area. The main dining room alone featured six chandeliers. There was the huge Cameo Ballroom with its wide doorways, intricately plastered ceiling, and ornate chandelier; the cozy North Parlor with huge fireplaces; the Victorian Writing Room, with its gold crest over the fireplace and two huge floor-to-ceiling windows framed by flowery drapes; the Clock Lobby, with one large clock in the middle of the wall; and all manner of shops. All the rooms—from the public areas to the guest suites—were brightly colored with the most extravagant drapes, paints, and fabrics in pink and green.

The hotel was also home to one of the finest bathhouses in the world. The swimming pool alone measured one hundred feet by forty-two feet and sat under a glass roof, surrounded by walkways lined with white columns. An inhalation room treated the respiratory system and asthma, and there were detoxifying baths using mud from the nearby springs. Then there were the grounds. The hotel had a golf course with rolling green hills. People traveled from the world over to play there. It also offered horseback riding along the resort's dirt trails, swimming in a huge outdoor pool, clay tennis courts, casino gambling, an antiques shop, and even a movie theater for the guests. Back then the Greenbrier was advertised as a "city under one roof."

All sorts of beautiful people stayed at the resort, all dressed formally—the men in tuxedos or suits and ties, the women in ball gowns. The movie star Clark Gable visited the hotel, and I once got to meet a duke and duchess from

England. Since the resort attracted guests internationally, we saw people from all over Europe.

During summers, Horace and Charlie often worked alongside Daddy as bellmen, wearing uniforms to work, carrying guests' steamer trunks up to their rooms, and responding to guests' requests. They'd also operate the elevators, ferrying people up and down the six floors. At some point they even purchased a car to use to chauffeur wealthy people around. When I was older, I joined Margaret in the valet shop, doing work like unpacking the guests' trunks and pressing their clothes, as well as babysitting their children.

I also worked in the antiques shop, cleaning and dusting things like the sets of beautiful Russian glasses that sat on the shelf.

These experiences gave us a peek into the lives of the "rich and famous" people of that era.

While the Greenbrier was open to Whites only, sometimes after-hours some of its amenities were made available to townsfolk. This included us. After eleven p.m. we could go to the movies at its private theater for about a dime. We were not allowed on the guest courts, but I learned to play tennis on the back courts, which had been allocated for the help to use.

Horace and Charlie occasionally played tennis with John and Bobby Kennedy, who stayed there many times. Unlike many of the other elite, who looked down their noses at everyday people, John and Bobby Kennedy acted normally. They would go on to become the president and attorney general of the United States, respectively.

Despite the apparent familiarity, Horace and Charlie always had to remember that they could play with the Kennedys but we were still Colored. That meant we could carry people's luggage through the front doors, but when we arrived at work, we were never to go through the main entrance.

On October 29 of 1929, the stock market crashed. I was just eleven years old, but I

Here I am in ninth grade.

will never forget the Great Depression, which lasted more than a decade. West Virginia was hit extremely hard. In some counties 80 percent of the population didn't have a job. Coal mining companies failed, and thousands of miners found themselves out of work and their families destitute. People who had migrated from their family farms to the coal camps and textile mills that had promised greater opportunity were forced to return home, including Colored men who had worked in the coal mines. (The textile industry had refused to hire Colored people.) There was no work back home, though, and people who had returned could do little more than raise the food they needed to feed their families. Lots of people just abandoned their farms and migrated to places like Baltimore and New York. The Works Progress Administration and the Public Works Administration provided men with work building things like roads, bridges, and schools. Though Colored people paid taxes, the schools that were built were for Whites only.

You might not have known what was happening by observing life at the Greenbrier, which continued to be upgraded and whose renovation was completed during the

1930s. But back home Daddy suffered as the banks failed and other Colored men lost their jobs and began competing with him for work. Everyone was poor. We all worked harder, cut back so that we bought just the necessities, and made our meals last longer. It was only by the grace of God that Daddy—and our family—survived.

Somehow, in the midst of all this, Daddy was able to keep me in high school at the Institute. I graduated in the spring of 1932 at age thirteen. That fall, when I was fourteen, I started college.

The professors and students were on a mission to help advance the cause of Colored people. Our professors knew us, had high expectations for us, and wanted us to excel because they knew what lay ahead of us professionally. No matter how educated you were back then, getting a job was a problem. Many Colored people with master's degrees and PhDs could not obtain work; in fact, some of the most educated men became Pullman porters, tending to White people riding the trains, many of whom were less educated than they were. Among Colored people there developed an adage: "You have to be twice as good in order to be thought of as half as good" as your White counterparts. And so that was our charge—to excel. Many of my fellow classmates viewed themselves as different from and perhaps even superior to the common Colored person. They drew a sharp distinction between themselves and the Colored people in the village of Institute, whom they deemed inferior and considered "farmers." Given my roots, this made me feel uncomfortable.

To help pay for my schooling, I began to work in President Davis's office, my willingness to learn typing over the previous summer paying off with a coveted office job. By then I was well known for being precocious—what today we might term "gifted."

I came to know all of the professors, and they knew me. Dr. Thorne headed the English department, Dr. Matheus headed the French department, and Dr. Evans headed the mathematics department while Dr. William W. Schieffelin Claytor, the third Colored man ever to earn a doctorate— the highest educational degree that anyone could earn— in math, was on leave from the mathematics department. Upon his return, Dr. Claytor ran the math department.

In fact, the Institute took pride in the fact that two math professors had PhDs while the all-White West Virginia University, which was supposed to be superior to the Institute, didn't have any. That made Dr. Claytor the first PhD—White or Colored—to teach math at any college in the state.

The summer following my freshman year, I was working in the small antiques shop at the Greenbrier, unpacking and pressing clothes from the guests' trunks, when one of the guests began speaking to her husband in French. Sister and I would often unpack guests' clothes and then tell Mama about the dresses, knowing that she could imitate some of the details.

I looked up from my pressing and began to listen.

The woman's voice was spirited, and her hands gestured gracefully. I saw the woman, whose name was Countess Sala, look at me, so I looked away. But she was so intriguing that I inconspicuously looked back. She caught my eye. Suddenly the conversation stopped.

"You understood everything I was saying, didn't you?" Countess Sala said to me.

A part of me worried that I was going to get in trouble. But I remembered what Daddy always used to tell us: "You are no better than anyone else, but nobody else is better than you."

So I looked her in the eye and said, "Yes, ma'am, I did."

She walked toward me, her high heels clicking across the marble floor. I could smell her perfume.

"How did you learn to understand French?" she asked me.

"I learned it in school," I answered.

"Where do you go to school?"

"I attend the West Virginia Colored Institute, ma'am."

"What's your name?" she asked inquisitively.

"Katherine Coleman, ma'am," I answered.

"How old are you?"

"I'm sixteen, ma'am."

"Well, isn't that something. Good for you. You are only sixteen years old and you understand French well enough to know what I'm talking about, yet the rest of the people in this hotel only know enough French to order wine and foie gras."

I didn't know what "foie gras" meant.

Then she turned and walked away.

"This girl speaks French," she said to no one in particular. "It's a shame that she has no one to speak it with, being Colored." Then she disappeared. I never saw her again.

Later that week I was unpacking a trunk when one of the managers approached me.

"Are you Katherine Coleman?" the man asked.

"Yes, sir, I am."

"The chef would like to see you."

"The chef?"

"Yes, the chef," the messenger told me. "He would like to speak with you."

"Now?" I asked. "I'm supposed to be unpacking this trunk and pressing the guest's clothes."

I looked at my supervisor.

"You can go," she said.

I followed the man to the dining room and into the kitchen, a huge room with large brass cauldrons hanging from the ceiling, pots steaming on several stoves, ovens humming, and men wearing white aprons and chef's hats scurrying around very busily.

There was one man—a White man with a bit of a belly—who was shouting out instructions that everyone seemed to be listening to. We walked up to him.

"Here is the girl," said the man who'd come to get me.

The other man looked down at me. "You're Katherine Coleman?" he asked.

"Yes, sir."

"*Parlez-vous français?*" he asked.

"*Oui, monsieur. Un peu,*" I answered, telling him that I spoke French a little bit.

"Where did you learn French?" he asked me in French.

"At school," I answered.

The chef smiled. "You understand quite a bit, I see."

"I love French," I told him. "I love to read and write, and I like to learn."

"Well, how would you like to learn French from me?"

I gasped, and my hands flew up and covered my open mouth!

"*Me?!*"

"Yes," he said. "Would you like to speak French with me?"

"I'd like that, sir," I responded politely, though deep down inside I couldn't believe my good fortune.

"If you will come here every Monday at seven a.m.,

I will speak French with you, and you will surprise your teacher in the fall when you go back to school."

"Thank you very much, sir. I'd like that."

If I could have skipped back to my work, I would have. But that would have been improper, and I didn't want to be scolded for misbehaving.

So every Monday morning I got up early and practiced French with the chef. The chef and I grew to love our exchanges, and I fell in love with French.

That summer I stopped calling my mother "Mama" and started calling her "Mamá" with a French accent. Somehow the name stuck, and that's what everyone started calling her.

When I returned to school that fall, my teacher asked me if I had traveled to France, my French was so improved.

I loved the intrigue of a foreign language, so I figured I would major in French. French made me imagine the exotic places I was learning about. By then the chef had exposed me to the exciting flavors and sauces of French cuisine, and I'd developed a taste for them. I imagined myself teaching French to Colored children. Maybe one day they would have a chance to visit France. Perhaps I would too.

Of course, I also took the other required classes—math, science, Latin, physics, literature, history, and so on. I enjoyed literature a lot. I was also attracted to the math and science courses. The learning environment was very fertile.

Apparently, word traveled to Dr. Claytor by way of some of my professors that I was quite good in math. I was walking across campus during the first semester of my sophomore year when I saw him approaching on the walk.

"Katherine Coleman," he said, slowing down as he came closer.

"Hello, Dr. Claytor," I replied as I stopped.

"Have you declared your major yet?"

"I'm planning to major in French, sir."

"French, huh? I see. . . ."

"Yes, sir. I was being tutored by a French chef at the Greenbrier Hotel back in White Sulphur Springs."

"Well, that's mighty impressive, young lady," he said. "I have been away, but I am coming back to campus to teach math this year. If you're not in my class, I will come and find you."

I laughed that this famous professor knew me.

"I'm very serious," he continued.

"Well, then, I will major in both French and math."

Later that day I told Mamá about the conversation. She didn't want me to major in math. She wanted me to become a teacher. Unlike other positions afforded to Colored people, where the pay was low and the work was demeaning, teachers were well respected by the community. Not only that, but Colored teachers could make sixty-five dollars a month. (White teachers made one hundred dollars.) But it was almost unheard of for a Colored person to have a job in math or the sciences. On top of that, I was a woman.

Dr. Claytor was an excellent teacher. He would walk into the classroom, take a piece of chalk out of his pocket, go straight to the blackboard, and begin.

By then I'd really grown to love math—its simplicity, its elegance, how in a world rife with the dangers of racism and economic uncertainty, it provided clear-cut answers: Either you were right or you were wrong. The answer today was the same as it would be tomorrow. Dr. Evans had me

Professor James C. Evans with his grandson.

take every math class the school offered. He and Dr. Claytor even taught me a couple of extra classes.

Then one day Dr. Claytor asked me to stay after class. "You would be a good research mathematician," he told me, "and I'm going to see to it that you're prepared to become one."

"What do they do?" I asked him.

"You'll find out!"

"Where will I get a job?"

"That will be your problem," he said. I laughed at his wordplay. I already excelled at solving equations in math. I guessed I would solve this problem too.

From then on that's what I wanted to be.

Now, many professors will tell you that you'd be good at this or that, but they don't necessarily help you with the career path. Dr. Claytor made sure I was ready by ensuring that I took all of the math classes I'd need. Then he went above and beyond, developing some classes just for me. For instance, he created a class about the geometry of outer space. We studied the lines, angles, orbits, and shapes of outer space. I was so far ahead of the other students, I often found myself taking his courses alone.

When I finished my classes, I'd go to President Davis's office to work. I'd go to the library to study or to tutor a student who was struggling. At first the fact that I was so young yet helping an older student seemed to attract a lot of attention. But I treated all my schoolmates the same; I didn't look down on kids who didn't know as much as I did. I liked them all and just tried to help. After a while I simply blended in with everyone else and nobody paid me any mind. When the day ended, I'd head home, walking across the grassy lawns of the campus at twilight, then winding my way through town until I arrived.

The Institute was a center where Colored people's aspirations to fully participate in American society were entertained. It had recently been accredited to offer four-year degrees and had come to be called West Virginia State College. (In 2004 it would become a university, offering graduate education.) We students imagined ourselves the teachers and leaders of Colored society. We debated whether we should follow the philosophy of W. E. B. Du Bois, a great sociologist, historian, and founder of the civil rights organization the National Association for the Advancement of Colored People (NAACP). Du Bois believed that one in every ten Colored men ought to become leaders, so they needed the same classical education that White men received. Back then a college education was seen almost exclusively as something for White men. Dr. Du Bois was in an ongoing debate with Booker T. Washington, former president of the famous Tuskegee Institute in Alabama, who believed that Colored people should obtain a practical education that would allow them to work as craftsmen or farmers, the trades they were most likely to have. Famous speakers and artists such as George Washington Carver, Benjamin Mays, Paul Robeson, and Marian Anderson came to our campus.

During 1934, I was invited to join Alpha Kappa Alpha Sorority, Incorporated (AKA). There were three sororities and three fraternities when I was on campus. You had to have good grades and a high moral character to be invited. To apply, or pledge, I was required to learn the chapter's history and what I could do to help in the community. During the final weeks of the pledge process, we learned songs that taught us our sense of mission as well as brought us closer to one another. We ate, dressed, and pledged together. I loved being part of a community of women who would come together to improve the world.

Campus was a very exciting place to be.

We celebrated when the famous track athlete Jesse Owens won four gold medals at the 1936 Olympics in Berlin, Germany, delivering a sharp rebuke to Adolf Hitler's Nazism and belief in the White supremacy of a subset of Germans called Aryans. We cheered when Joe Louis, who was known as the Brown Bomber, was named the Athlete of the Year by the Associated Press. In 1937, he would become the first Negro world champion in boxing—and the first Negro to be widely admired by White Americans.

Students rolled up their sleeves and got involved in the campaign to end racial violence against Colored people, including lynchings. Mobs and even communities of angry Whites used terror to enforce the norms of segregation. Colored people might be hung, shot, dragged from the back of a vehicle, or burned alive for things like refusing to empty their pockets, addressing a White police officer without using the title "mister," or knocking on the door of a White woman's house. This drove Colored Americans to migrate north to greater safety.

Virginia had been among the states where the most lynchings took place, with 88 people lynched by violent gangs between 1880 and 1940. During that time, neighboring North Carolina had 122. So students were passionate about the issue. Young people were inspired by the activists and suffragettes Ida B. Wells and Mary Church Terrell, who led anti-lynching campaigns beginning in the 1890s after one of their friends was lynched. The anti-lynching movement came to a head in 1935, four years after Ida B. Wells died, when two senators proposed federal anti-lynching laws. The legislation didn't pass—indeed, lynching didn't become a federal crime until 2018—but the number of lynchings dropped dramatically during the 1930s. Students also involved themselves in the movement to gain equal rights, in voter registration and participation drives, and in state and national politics. Though many of the students helped to raise the food in the Institute's gardens, we also complained about the quality and limited quantity of food in the dining hall.

In 1937, at age eighteen, I graduated from West Virginia State *summa cum laude* with degrees in mathematics and French. I had earned the highest grade-point average of any student during the first forty-six years of the school's existence. And because I'd been skipped forward so many years, I graduated one year before both Horace and Charlie and only two years after Margaret. Back then I believed that the guys were slow learners. Sometimes I felt sorry for them. Today I understand that they were very bright. Indeed, Margaret and Charlie would go on to earn master's degrees in education, one at Columbia University and the other at

New York University. Years later both Horace and Charlie would serve our nation in the military. Sister would teach elementary school in West Virginia, and Charlie would become a principal, then administrator in North Carolina.

Though it had been difficult, and despite long odds and months spent apart, Mamá and Daddy's vision for our family was successful. Having all four children obtain both high school and college degrees was a feat that would have made any family proud—Northern or Southern, Colored, White, or anything else. This reflected both uncommon vision and a heroic level of sacrifice on my parents' part. However, their sacrifices were also typical of the determination that Colored people exhibited so that their children could get an education during an era when many states intended to deny them one and limit their access to opportunity.

Me (center) at my college graduation.

# CHAPTER 3

That fall of 1937, I started my first teaching assignment. It was a desperate time during that Depression era. Fortunately, some demand existed for Colored educators. Back then, when a Colored school needed a teacher, the principal would provide the state's Colored college with the school's requirements, and the college would send a list of recent graduates who possessed those qualifications. Carnegie Elementary School in Marion, Virginia, needed a teacher who could teach both math and music. Since I fit the bill, I was offered the assignment.

As in most Southern states, Virginia's public schools were segregated by race. During that era, most White

Virginians thought that if Colored people became educated, they would challenge the existing social order,
which was rooted in White supremacy—the belief that
White people were genetically superior to non-White
people, including Colored people. (By then many of us—
though not all—had stopped calling ourselves "Colored,"
a term that had been assigned to us by White people and
which many of us associated with slavery. Instead, some
of us had begun calling ourselves "Negroes," a term more
of our choosing, though still not perfect. Today the word
"Negro" has been replaced by "African American" and
"Black," as each generation has sought to describe us in
ways that affirm ourselves and that reject labels applied to
us by people who have oppressed us.)

Most White southerners believed that if Negroes
became well educated, we would no longer allow White
people to underpay or exploit us, no matter the job—
whether as teachers or nurses, the jobs that more educated
women might have, or as domestic servants, farmworkers,
and laborers, which were often the only options available
for everyone else. Whites feared that we would fight for

equal rights and equal participation in American society instead. Frankly, they were probably right. What they didn't understand, though, was that a well-educated society is not only morally right, but makes life better for everyone. Many White people also feared that we would seek revenge and be as cruel to them as they had been to us.

The government, which was controlled solely by White people, intentionally deprived Colored schools of funding even though it taxed Colored people. It also paid Negro teachers far less than White teachers. Segregation was humiliating, but we dealt with it as we pressed for change in various ways, large and small.

What Colored schools did have going for them was a dedicated cadre of Negro educators and students hungry to learn. Though school systems paid Colored teachers less, they typically required Colored teachers to possess a greater level of training than the White teachers had. The higher requirements were intended to discourage Colored people from becoming teachers—and that worked. But this also meant that Negro teachers tended to be more highly educated than White teachers were. Additionally, colleges for Colored people instilled students with a tremendous sense of purpose: to help lift the Colored race so that we could fully participate in American society. So when Whites would announce that high school entrance exams would take place the next day in a different part of the state, as often happened to keep us from attending, the community would move heaven and earth to get their children there.

That said, life for Colored people during the era of racial segregation was both humiliating and dangerous. From water fountains to bathrooms, swimming pools and beaches, buses and trains, and schools, public facilities were designated either for White people or for Colored people. If we wanted to eat at a Whites-only restaurant, we had to go to the back door and order takeout. And the danger of lynching, though subsiding, remained. The Ku Klux Klan lurked as a constant threat, and resentful Whites were ever present.

So while attending inferior schools was humiliating, doing so also protected us from some of the violent threats, demeaning taunts, and racial slurs that Colored people commonly faced during segregation.

* * * * * * * * *

Marion was a small, idyllic town of about fifty-five hundred people set in the lush, tree-covered mountains of southwestern Virginia near the Hungry Mother State Park. Named for Revolutionary War hero Francis Marion, the town's claim to fame when I lived there was Marion College, a two-year Lutheran women's college. As did life in much of the area, the region's economy centered around coal mining.

The town of Marion was overwhelmingly White; only about 150 of the families were Colored. The Colored people were pretty much all related to one another, and most of their families were very large. With thirteen children, the Goble family was the largest of all. In fact, two of the Goble children were in my class.

Most of the White families in Marion weren't wealthy, but they had far more money than did the Colored people, who were barely scraping by. White women hired Colored women as housekeepers and domestics. Colored men found jobs as carpenters, brickmasons, janitors, shoeshiners, handymen, and yard workers. They also did other dirty, dangerous, or menial jobs. There had been a number of tobacco farms in the region, where Colored people had worked going all the way back to slavery. But by the time I moved there, the tobacco industry was in decline.

To improve their economic prospects, many Colored men would seek work elsewhere. They would labor in places like the state capital, Richmond, or on the C&O Railway that ran between the Chesapeake Bay and the Ohio River and beyond, or in Norfolk, along the Virginia coast, where the big military installations, like Langley Air Force Base, Hampton Roads, and the Norfolk naval station were located.

Indeed, it wasn't unusual for five or six men to squeeze into a car or onto the back of a truck to drive to a job that was located as far as eight hours away. The men would stay there all week or perhaps even two, typically rooming with relatives or other Colored families, who would open their homes and charge for rooms and meals. The mothers and children back at home would lean on one another and on other family members while their husbands and fathers were away. Another common scenario would be for one person to settle in a more promising place and other family members to follow one by one. Each new member would get a job in the new place and send money home so the next family member could join them. Colored families and communities were always engaged in self-help and sacrificing in order to move forward so that the next generation would have better opportunities.

Though Marion looked quaint and idyllic from the outside, the city's Colored residents knew to stay in their place. The threat of violence was never far off. At least five public hangings of Colored people by White lynch mobs had taken place in Virginia during the 1920s alone. A particularly grisly lynching took place in 1926. It wasn't until 1928 that the state passed an anti-lynching law. Fear of being hung or having their homes or businesses burned down kept Colored people feeling frightened.

Negroes faced indignities at every turn. Mr. Charles Goble, the father of the thirteen children, was a Colored barber, but he couldn't cut Colored men's or even his own sons' hair in his barbershop. When Negroes wanted to get an ice-cream cone, we couldn't enter the front door of the pharmacy; we had to go around back. Colored people had to sit in the balcony of the movie theater, often disparagingly called the "peanut gallery." Negroes both worked within the system as best they could and resisted it in ways large and small—from declining to answer when someone White called us a disparaging name, to engaging in strikes and refusing to work. At the movies, sometimes the Colored children would demonstrate their displeasure by throwing pieces of popcorn over the railing onto the White people sitting below.

Colored adults would try to protect their children from racism's danger and indignities by doing things like making ice cream at home, holding picnics, throwing parties and gatherings in our own homes, creating parallel clubs and organizations for Colored people, and even freezing our own outdoor skating rink. Having separate activities was far safer than attempting to integrate anything.

Yet the rules of segregation could also be fickle. Though the schools were segregated, sometimes Colored and White children would play together after classes let out, as they had when we'd lived back at Dutch Run. Or a White woman might give the Black woman who cleaned her home a piece of furniture that she was discarding or a hand-me-down dress for the Black woman's daughter to wear to a social.

The Carnegie Elementary School was a little two-story red building that sat up on a hill. Rumor had it that the school had been funded by the wealthy industrialist Andrew Carnegie. He had become a major donor to the Tuskegee Institute in Alabama. He was also among a handful of philanthropists who helped to fund the education of the nation's Colored citizens.

Carnegie Elementary started at kindergarten, but like so many other schools for Colored children during that era, it didn't go all the way through high school. There were about fifteen children in every grade. The school's teachers had migrated from all over the region to educate them. In addition to math, I taught music. A violin teacher would come all the way from Roanoke, Virginia, more than one hundred miles away. The children were like sponges, eager for knowledge.

But after they graduated from seventh grade, Colored children who wanted to continue their education had to leave home to attend the Petersburg Normal School for Negroes. The Petersburg school was 268 miles away. Very few people could afford to live away from their family in order to continue their schooling. For the few families whose children were able to go, Colored people in the community shared resources and pooled their money to help young people attend. Every Colored person in town went to the train station to see the children off as they took the Norfolk and Western Railway line to Petersburg to attend school.

On the other hand, White children went to high school in the area. That's how unfair things were during that era and why Colored people fought so hard and engaged in so much self-help in an effort to achieve equality.

One of the first things I noticed was that, for such a small community, a lot of the Colored children somehow found a way to go on to college. In one class, five of the thirteen students sought to advance their education. That was a lot even when compared to a White school. Years after I left the area, four of my former students would attend Virginia State College.

In some families the oldest child would forgo college in order to work so that a younger child could continue his or her education. In other families the older children would go to college in hopes that they could help provide for their younger siblings. Negroes may not have had much money or opportunity, but spiritually, financially, and emotionally, everyone pulled everyone else along. We took turns opening doors for one another.

I showed up in town excited to have my very first job. Like most of the other teachers who came from out of town, I became a boarder in another person's home. Mrs. Gert Ross rented me a bedroom in her house and cooked dinner for me.

I couldn't wait for school to start.

I will always remember my first day as a teacher. I put on my high heels, a gray A-line dress that I had made myself, and a little bit of lipstick. (I wouldn't learn until later that in Marion it was considered outrageous for a teacher to wear lipstick.) I taught my students to love mathematics. They learned about multiples of ten and tricks for multiplying by nine by using their fingers. I taught them how to use rulers, compasses, protractors, and triangular scales. I shared my love of x and y variables, and of integers, decimal points, and fractions. We drew arcs, rhombuses, parallelograms, and curves. I loved my students, and they loved me.

Back then, just as today, some teachers merely taught right and wrong answers. I don't agree with that approach. I taught students to understand the background of what they were working on, how to figure out what the problem was and then how to attack it. Because if you approach any problem properly, you'll get the answer. If you don't get it the first time, you'll get it the second time. In the meantime, you'll experience the joy of learning and have the tremendous satisfaction that comes with figuring something out on your own. That is much better than just solving the question on a test.

I taught my students to be curious. You see, if you lose your curiosity, then you stop learning.

At some point during the semester, I was asked to put on a play to raise money for the school. The play, a comedy, included a womanless wedding in which all of the participants were men. Some men had to play women's parts and dress up like women.

I was going to play the piano, but I needed somebody who could sing.

I asked around since I was new and didn't know anyone. "What man around here has a decent singing voice?"

"I know someone who can sing," said one of my colleagues. "His name is Jimmie Goble, and he just moved home after graduating from college."

"Oh, I have one of the Goble girls, Pat, in my class," I replied.

So I called Jimmie Goble that evening when I went home.

"Hello. My name is Katherine Coleman. I'm one of the teachers at Carnegie Elementary School."

"Hello, Miss Coleman. How can I help you?"

"Do you know 'I Love You Truly'?" I asked, knowing that depending upon how he interpreted my question we might have a little fun.

"Why, Miss Coleman, you don't know me well enough to say that to me," he joked.

We laughed, and I explained what I needed. I have to admit that I was flirting a little. Who was this man who had just come home from college?

When he came to rehearsal that weekend, we hit it off

right away. He told me to call him Jimmie. (Later I learned that all the Gobles had nicknames for one another and his family called him Snook.)

He was about my color and of average height with big beautiful brown eyes and a receding hairline.

Jimmie was five years older than me. He had graduated from Lincoln University in Missouri, where he had majored in science, with an interest in biology. The Goble family was very educated. Most of them had attended college. One of his siblings went to Knoxville State, three had gone to Lincoln, and the rest went to Virginia State College, all Colored schools. His family was like my family in that both families would go to any extent to send their children to college.

Because both he and I had attended college, we discovered we had a lot of experiences in common. In addition, both of us came from families that taught us to help others. His father had taught that, insofar as their education was concerned, each of the children was responsible for helping the next child get through.

Both of us were also musically inclined. He sang bass, and I sang soprano. He played brass instruments: trumpet, trombone, and tuba, as well as the flute. I played the piano. We both had a good sense of humor. I already knew his family through the school. And both of us had sisters named Margaret.

One day, months after the play was over, Jimmie asked, "Katherine Coleman, might I come calling on you this Sunday after church?"

"Why, yes, I would like that!"

So that Sunday afternoon, he walked me home after church and we sat on the front porch laughing, drinking fresh sweet tea with lemon, and talking for hours. We talked about the dust bowl in the Great Plains, where he'd attended college; the tragic crash of the Hindenburg blimp; and concert vocalist Marian Anderson's performance before more than seventy-five thousand people on the steps of the Lincoln Memorial.

Whether we sat on the porch, walked through the hills, or went to the movies or for a drive, when Jimmie and I were together, everything was just easy and natural.

He'd met my parents when they'd come to visit and, as I'd expected, they'd liked him.

Then, one day, he looked at me with a glimmer in his eye.

"Miss Katherine Coleman, I wonder if you would consider marrying me?"

"Yes, Jimmie Goble, I would!" I told him. "But I have to ask my father first."

"Hello. Operator . . ."

"Yes, I'm trying to reach two-two-eight, please."

"Oh, the Colemans," the operator said. "Please hold . . ."

*Ring . . . Ring . . . Ring . . .*

Where were they?

The phone rang nine times before my mother finally picked up.

"Mamá, I have something I want to talk to you and Daddy about."

"Hold on just a moment," she told me. "I was washing dishes and my hands are still wet, and your father, he's out back trimming the apple tree."

"Well, will you go get him?"

"Hold on now . . ."

I could hear Mamá call Daddy and his faint reply. It

seemed like forever until she finished drying her hands and picked up the telephone again.

"What's going on, Katherine?" she asked. "What do you want to tell me?"

"The young man you met when you were here visiting? Well, he has asked me to marry him, Mamá!"

"Oh, Katherine, how exciting!" she said. "He seems like a wonderful young man."

"Yes, Mamá, and he comes from a wonderful family. I'm calling to ask your permission."

"Well, you have my blessings, Katherine," Mamá told me. I had expected as much, but I was relieved. Now I just needed to tell my father. If only he would hurry up and get on the line!

Finally, I could hear his boots step onto the back porch.

"Katherine?"

"Hey, Daddy!"

"How are you doing? Is everything okay?"

"Daddy, I'm calling you to ask your permission. Jimmie Goble asked me to marry him!"

I'd thought my father would quickly congratulate me and give me his blessings. Instead what I heard was a silence so deep and long, you would have thought I had called home to tell him that I was pregnant.

"Well, what do you think?" I finally asked.

"Katherine, I'm sorry, but I don't want you to marry this young man."

"*What?!*" I felt my face heat up. "I don't understand."

"Well—"

"Well, what?" I interrupted. "I've done everything you've asked me, Daddy."

"I know."

"I studied hard, I finished school, and I got a job just like you said. And now I've found a good man that I love and I want to marry."

"Yes, sweetheart, that's true."

"Then why don't you want me to marry him, Daddy?"

"Katherine, there are just some things that you have to trust your father about."

"Trust?" I asked. "I trust you, but you have to tell me— what are you talking about?"

"Well, I really can't say," he said. "Sometimes you just have to trust your father. . . ."

I saw Jimmie almost every day. I knew him to be a faithful, accomplished, and honest man. What in heaven's name was Daddy talking about?

My mind was made up.

"Well," I interrupted. "I'm getting married. I won't ask you again."

With that, I said goodbye and hung up the phone.

On Thursday, November 9, 1939, I slipped into the high-necked white wedding dress with short sleeves that my mother had sewn for me, and Jimmie donned a black suit and bow tie. Mamá pinned a beautiful corsage on me.

Then Jimmie and I stood in front of God and vowed to love each other until death do us part. Afterward we held a reception for our

Our wedding day!

families and friends, and I cut our beautiful three-level white wedding cake with white frosting and put a bite into Jimmie's mouth, playfully getting a little frosting on his face. He did the same with me. Daddy hadn't wanted us to marry, but he attended, as I'd known he would. He seemed a little distant, though; I always wondered why.

Jimmie and I took the next day off from work and began

Jimmie and I cutting our wedding cake.

our lives together, renting a couple of rooms in the home of the Dabney family, where we would live.

On Monday morning I went right back to work. Schools preferred that women teachers be single, since they assumed that once the women married, they would soon be pregnant, so I knew that the school wouldn't be as happy about our wedding as we were. Jimmie had just returned home and was still seeking a job, so we needed to be cautious.

Back then women didn't keep their own names or hyphenate them. It wasn't even considered, and any woman who even suggested it would have been thought of as disrespecting her husband. I returned to work and told my students to now call me Mrs. Goble.

But I wouldn't stay in Marion long.

President Davis at the Institute was sitting in his office when he received a call. It was Dr. Charles Elmer Lawall, the president of West Virginia University, the state's all-White college.

"We are about to be sued," he told President Davis.

"Why is that?" President Davis replied.

"We are being forced to integrate," President Lawall said. "I'm wondering if you can send me some of your top students for our graduate program."

"I imagine I can help you, President Lawall," President Davis said, feeling excited about the opportunity to open doors for and showcase some of his best students, but also resentful that the all-White school had needed external pressure.

"I have two gentlemen who have graduated recently and are already principals," President Davis said. "I would also suggest a very brilliant young woman who just got her diploma, Katherine Coleman. She's a mathematician and earned the highest GPA we've ever had here."

I was thrilled when the offer was extended to me. It was an honor to be selected to be among the first Colored students to integrate a university.

So at the end of my first year of teaching, I packed up my belongings and traveled the roughly two hundred fifty miles to Morgantown for the summer to begin graduate school at West Virginia University.

West Virginia University is located along the banks of the mighty Monongahela River, which flows from the Allegheny Mountains in West Virginia to the Ohio River near Pittsburgh—one of the few rivers in the world that flow from south to north. The campus looked a lot like the Institute, with its rolling hills, redbrick Victorian buildings, and bluestone roofs.

I understood that integration might not be easy. I might be spit on or threatened or have rocks thrown at me. I was nervous, but it came with the territory. I wanted the opportunity.

Several days before the school year began, I moved in with a family on the Colored side of town. On the first day of class, I put on my navy-blue dress and practical shoes and walked over to campus. Once I reached the math building, I met my adviser, a White man, for the first time. I no longer remember his name, but I do recall that he didn't seem too happy to see me.

"What are you going to do with this advanced degree?" he asked, staring down over the top of his spectacles.

"I'm going to be a research mathematician," I answered.

"What is that?" he asked condescendingly.

"I don't know, but it's what I'm going to do and I'm going to find out."

"And what are you going to do to provide for yourself until then?"

"I'm probably going to do the same thing you do: teach," I said nonchalantly.

The idea that a Colored woman could in any way be his equal seemed to not sit well with him. His face slowly turned the color of one of the Greenbrier's French roses. I hadn't particularly been trying to make a statement. I was just presenting the facts. I was no better than anyone, but I was no worse. This man wasn't going to get the best of me.

Even though I wasn't exactly sure yet what a research mathematician was, I loved math and wanted to become one.

Fortunately, my classmates didn't seem to be bothered by my presence.

But by the end of the summer session, I was missing Jimmie. And stronger than my desire to obtain my doctorate in math, I had started feeling the urge to have a baby. Everywhere I went I noticed women with babies. I started counting the number of infants I saw every day. I found myself cooing at and falling in love with every child that passed by. I knew the time had come to start a family. So I didn't return to West Virginia University for the fall semester. Instead I returned to Marion and resumed teaching, this time alongside Jimmie, who had also begun teaching at Carnegie Elementary.

That September, while I was dreaming about babies, a German battleship opened fire on Polish troops. Then more than 1.5 million German troops stormed over the Polish border, sparking the onset of World War II.

# CHAPTER 4

**L**ittle did any of us understand how a war that was fought primarily in Europe would have such a drastic effect on all of our lives.

On December 7, 1941, Japanese kamikaze fighter planes, dive bombers, and torpedo bombers attacked Pearl Harbor in Hawaii. The Japanese destroyed or damaged three navy cruisers, three destroyers, an anti-aircraft training ship, and one minelayer, leading our nation into World War II. One hundred eighty-eight US aircraft were destroyed. More than twenty-four hundred Americans were killed and almost twelve hundred people were wounded. Our nation was now at war.

In response, President Roosevelt signed legislation that required roughly 120,000 Japanese Americans to be forcibly relocated into military isolation camps in California, Oregon, and Washington State. They were required to stay there from 1942 to 1945—a horrible violation of their human rights. The government interred Japanese, German, and other diplomats from enemy countries at the Greenbrier, of all places—both to keep the diplomats from leaving the country and to make sure that they were treated well. Eventually some German prisoners of war would stay there. The Greenbrier also became the place where the government would keep the US Congress safe in the event of a nuclear Armageddon.

In addition to increasing Americans' fears, World War II had a profound effect upon our family. All of Jimmie's brothers were drafted into the military. Everyone except him. He hadn't passed the physical. He had started getting headaches, though they were minor at the time.

Both Horace and Charlie joined the military as well. Charlie served at Fort Eustis, the transportation headquarters for the entire army, where all the soldiers would ship out for their assignments. When the military found out how intelligent he was and that he could write and was good at math, he had a leg up over most everyone else. The commander immediately made Charlie his secretary. Charlie would go on to become a master sergeant.

Horace was the more mechanical of the two and would serve overseas.

The entire nation sacrificed. More than 45 percent of women worked outside the home during the war, producing ammunition, building ships and airplanes, driving trains, and nursing the wounded. Suddenly there was a demand for faster planes; however, the war made clear the reality that the nation had fallen behind Europe in aviation.

It was just an ordinary day in late April—a little bit cloudy with some sprinkles here and there. But I will never forget it because that was the first time I missed my monthly cycle. I didn't really feel any different. Could I actually be pregnant?

I called my mother to ask. She told me that I was probably pregnant, but not to tell anyone except Jimmie. Back then, once a woman was with child, oftentimes she wasn't allowed to work. People believed that pregnant women were more fragile than we now know they are.

Being from such a large and close-knit family, Jimmie was particularly excited. Was it a boy? Would it be a girl? Neither of us could know until the baby was born. But we would share our daydreams aloud.

"He's going to have your brown eyes!"

"She's going to have your sense of humor."

"He's going to have your singing voice."

"She's going to be smart like you are, Katherine."

"Maybe our child will even be the first Negro president of the United States!"

For now we kept our fantasies to ourselves. If either of us—and especially Jimmie—let the cat out of the bag, the grapevine of gossip would spread the word. Then the whole town would know, and I would lose my job.

By the time I missed my second cycle, we were certain I was pregnant. Each morning, Jimmie would roll over and tell me that he'd had yet another dream about children.

"I think it's a girl, Katherine," he would tell me.

"Now, how would you know? I'm not even showing yet."

"I keep seeing little girls laughing in my dreams, and I have this feeling inside."

We made a list of names, but decided that if it was a girl, we'd name her Joylette, after Mamá. A boy we decided we would name after Jimmie's father.

Though you couldn't yet tell by the way my clothes fit, Jimmie said he could look at my face and tell that I was full of new life. We hid the pregnancy for as long as we could.

Fortunately, since Jimmie had a college degree, the principal invited him to replace me in my classroom when the time came.

A neighbor of Mrs. Goble's became my midwife.

Mamá would come to visit every couple of weeks.

"I can tell by how you're carrying," she told me during the final months as she looked at my growing belly. "It's going to be a girl."

And Daddy? Well, he may not have wanted me to marry Jimmie, but he was tickled pink at the idea that I was carrying Jimmie's child and that he was about to become a grandfather.

On December 27, 1940, I woke up feeling parts of my

body that I hadn't even known existed start to spasm and contract as my body entered a new phase of the miraculous process of creating new life. Jimmie and I went to his parents' house, where his mother, several of his sisters, and the midwife tended to me. The men stayed downstairs.

Jimmie and Mamá turned out to be right. Finally, at 11:40 that night I gave birth to a healthy baby girl. She was bald, weighed about seven pounds, and was nineteen inches tall. And when they placed her in my arms, I immediately fell in love in a way I'd never known before. Joylette didn't cry or need to be held, as some babies did. She seemed very independent from birth.

After that school year ended, we spent the summer in White Sulphur and decided to stay there so I could be close to my family and live in the community in which I'd been raised.

Joylette and I on our porch.

Jimmie accepted an offer to teach at the Tazewell County School in Bluefield, Virginia, located eighty miles to the south. He would instruct high school sciences, lead the band, and coach both the football and basketball teams. For about five years we lived in White Sulphur while he commuted back and forth. I stayed home taking care of Joylette, falling in love with her infectious laugh, her baby spit bubbles, and her tiny little hands.

Our family continued growing.

Our second daughter, Constance, was born on April 27, 1943, in my parents' home on Church Street. We named her after my dear childhood friend, Constance Davis, whom we'd affectionately called Dit. Joylette would walk up and down the street inviting people to see her new baby, whom we immediately started calling Connie.

Our youngest child was born less than one year after that, on April 17, 1944, ten days before Connie's first birthday. We were wondering if we might have a boy; we got a girl, whom we decided to name after me but call Kathy. She was a good baby too.

Everyone wanted to play with our girls. Charlie, who

Our three beautiful girls.

didn't have children of his own, always joked that we could give Kathy to him.

"What are you gonna do with another one?" he'd joke.

There wasn't a better place for me to be as a young mother with a commuting husband than home in White Sulphur. Mamá lived several doors down, and Margaret would come home sometimes from her job in Washington, DC, and would help me with the girls. During that time I became friendly with a woman named Dot Vaughan and her family, who lived across the street from my parents' house during the summers. Her husband, Howard, worked at the Greenbrier with Daddy, and her daughter would sit on Mamá's lap. Mamá would read to her on the front porch.

But driving back and forth to Bluefield was very hard on Jimmie. I would especially worry about him during rainstorms, when the hairpin turns of the Appalachians became slick with water, and during the winter, when the roads could turn treacherous.

Yet I have fond memories of that time. The girls and I would often wake up and walk down to Mamá's house, where we'd join her and Daddy for a hot breakfast of scrambled eggs, grits, biscuits, and a cut of pork called fatback. We'd

often eat dinner together as well. During the evening we'd have some applesauce or homemade cake.

Church Street remained the center of Negro life. Everyone who worked at the Greenbrier, everyone who came home from college, everyone who went to

In White Sulphur Springs with Connie, Kathy, and Joylette.

church or wanted soul food for dinner came over our way. The community was vibrant and bustling with love as people walked from place to place—we didn't do as much driving back then as people do today. We had lots of visitors, and many friends fussed over the babies. It was a wonderful location to raise three little toddlers.

In 1947, Jackie Robinson became the first Negro player to break the color line in baseball, when owner Branch Rickey invited him to join the Brooklyn Dodgers and integrate what was then America's favorite sport.

That same year, once we thought the girls were old enough, we all relocated to Bluefield, Virginia, so Jimmie wouldn't have to do so much driving. Already we'd almost experienced a catastrophe. During a snowstorm, we were driving through the mountains with the girls when Jimmie slid off the road and into the drainage ditch. Fortunately, we were behind a bus that had also gone off the road and was in trouble. The bus driver had already called for help, but Jimmie wasn't sure that whoever came could also help us. So he got somebody on the bus to watch the girls while he and I crawled up the icy highway back to a service station to get some help for us.

Now, just so I don't confuse you, let me explain. There are two Bluefields. Bluefield, Virginia, was a small town of about four thousand people located across the state line from Bluefield, West Virginia, which had about twenty thousand residents. Named for the coalfields that had been found alongside the nearby Bluestone River, the Bluefields sat amid some of the largest deposits of bituminous coal in the world. Railroad cars regularly rumbled through the area, piled high with coal.

Since the 1890s the area's coalfields had attracted Colored people from the Deep South as well as European immigrants who were searching for work. As growing numbers of Colored people had migrated to the area over the previous decades, the importance of educating them had become increasingly clear. The Bluefield Colored Institute was on the West Virginia side. For decades, the Bluefield Colored Institute—which in 1943 was renamed Bluefield State College—had prepared Negro teachers to help educate the region's Colored children. So perhaps it wasn't so surprising that the West Virginia Bluefield was one-quarter Colored, while Bluefield, Virginia, was almost all White. Also, rumor had it that at some point in Bluefield, Virginia, crosses had been burned on a Colored man's property, terrifying families into leaving town.

The Tazewell County School was a two-story brick building, with the principal's office and grades one through five on the ground floor, and grades six and seven, plus the high school upstairs. I taught French and math and directed the choir; Jimmie taught science, chemistry, and biology. Both of us were upstairs. We each made sixty-five dollars a month, which was a good wage for Colored people during those days. Of course, White teachers made a lot more.

On Connie's first day of school, Kathy said, "Where is she going? I want to go." So I brought her along and she sat in the classroom with Connie.

Since Jimmie and I were teaching at the same school, everything we did, we did as a team. The instruments the band members played and the uniforms worn by the cheerleaders had been discarded by the White school across town. I sewed new skirts so that the fifteen or so majorettes could wear the same costumes as they accompanied the band. For our homecoming parade, Jimmie would drive a pickup truck through town with the band on the back, always more major-ettes than instruments. When he drove the football team on the bus to the games, our girls often came along. I traveled alone from time to time with the choir.

Our relationship was a true partnership. Unlike many couples of that era, where the man held all the power, we were equal in our decision-making. Whoever got home first put on the apron and started cooking. In fact, we both could cook, paint, wallpaper, sing, and dance—and we did things together. But since I was so good with numbers, I was the one who handled the money.

During the summers, we would relocate to Rocky Mount, North Carolina, where Jimmie and I would work as chauffeur and maid for the Belchers, a wealthy White family in the lumber industry. Our family would stay in the living quarters atop their garage, and Jimmie and I would cook for Mr. and Mrs. Belcher, serve their meals, and drive them around town. These were typical jobs that Negroes took in order to keep their families afloat and move their children ahead. But just as our parents were determined that we wouldn't work at the Greenbrier as adults, Jimmie and I were determined that our girls would go to college so that they'd never be White people's servants.

Sometimes the Belcher girls would play with our girls. One time Mr. Belcher sat Joylette atop a horse and was walking with her when the horse just took off, leaving Mr. Belcher behind. Joylette fell off and split the corner of her mouth open, but the hospital wouldn't take her because it was for Whites only. Even Mr. and Mrs. Belcher's clout couldn't get her in until the next day.

One night Mr. Belcher drove somewhere on his own. Some way or another, he was killed in a car accident. Though Jimmie had helped attend to Mr. Belcher, he'd also liked him. Jimmie was crushed by this loss.

In 1949, our second year at Tazewell, our family moved out of the home we'd been living in and into a two-room suite in a mansion once owned by a very wealthy White family. The Carsons, a Colored family, now owned it.

The house was so large that three generations of Carsons lived in it. The parlor, living room, dining room, and kitchen were downstairs. The Carsons lived on the first floor. Our family of five lived in a large bedroom on the second floor. Jimmie and I slept on one side of the room, and all three of the girls slept in a three-quarter-size fold-up bed on the other—two with their heads at one end of the bed and one with her head at the other end. There was another family sharing the second floor with us. They lived in a five-room apartment, but we rarely saw them. Mr. Carson, the grandfather, also lived on that floor with his own bedroom and bathroom.

The Carsons' home sat up on a hill. In front of the home there were thirty-six steps. You went up twenty steps, and then there was a landing. Then you went up another four steps to a landing, then three additional sets of four and you were finally on the porch. During the fall the girls would roll down the front lawn through the leaves. One year, a pile of leaves was so high that Connie climbed into it and we couldn't find her. She was in there having an asthma attack.

A merry Christmas with our girls.

Though we lived in Bluefield, a couple of weekends each month we would all pile into the car and go to see either the Coleman or the Goble grandparents. It was the best way we could balance our need for work with raising our children to know their grandparents.

We lived that way for two straight years. During January of the third year, Jimmie and I went to a wedding on the other side of town. We were there enjoying the party when an unsettledness started creeping through the crowd.

"What's going on?" I asked the person next to me.

"I don't know. . . ."

"I heard someone say there's a house on fire," another person answered.

"Where?" I asked.

"The old Carson mansion—Coach's house!" somebody yelled.

My heart felt like a bowling ball and just dropped into my stomach.

Jimmie was the coach. That meant our house!

Jimmie grabbed my hand, and we raced toward the door together, bumping into people along the way. When we reached the door, Jimmie saw a couple of his players.

"Coach, your house is on fire," one of them said. "We came to tell you."

We were so panicked that we ran right past our car and down the hill toward the smoke. Jimmie let go of my hand, and he and the football players ran ahead. When I got to the street, I saw smoke pouring out of the windows to our apartment and the fire truck in front of the house. Some of the other players were milling around.

"JOYLETTE! CONNIE! KATHY" I screamed. Barely

able to breathe, I could hardly make it up the thirty-six steps to the door.

"Back up, miss," one of the firefighters ordered me.

"MY LITTLE GIRLS ARE INSIDE!" I screamed. It was all I could do not to drop to my knees.

"No, ma'am, your children are fine. They're over there," he said, pointing toward the other side of the house.

That was the moment when Jimmie called my name.

"Katherine, the girls are over here! They're okay!"

I ran to them and hugged them close.

"Are you okay? Are you hurt? What happened?"

They were crying and smelled like smoke. Connie couldn't stop coughing. But I hugged and kissed them all over—our girls were alive!

Between coughs, the girls all started talking at once.

"We were asleep . . ."

"I heard Connie start coughing like she was choking, so I woke up . . ."

"Then the closet door burst open and smoke started pouring out. . . ."

"So we woke Kathy up and . . ."

"I ran downstairs to tell the Carsons that there was smoke. . . ."

"Then they came up and got us out and moved us to the other side of the house. . . ."

"Then we had to get the grandfather, who was blind, out of the house. . . ."

Before long one of the neighbors came to where we were standing.

"Bring the girls over to our house," she said. "They can stay with us while you get things all sorted out."

Boy, were we grateful!

So the football players carried the girls down all thirty-six stairs to the neighbors' house.

While the girls spent the night at the neighbors', Jimmie and I waited until the firemen said it was safe; then we went into our room and saw the mess. The windows were open and the biting nighttime January wind whipped the curtains around. Soot covered everything. As we stood in the doorway, we could see our clothes and other items—most of them were destroyed. We spent the entire night sifting through our belongings, which the firemen had strewn around the bedroom or had gotten wet as they'd tried to fight the fire. We attempted to figure out what could be washed or cleaned or salvaged.

"Jimmie, do you see our diplomas?"

"No, baby, not yet. Oh, look at my Sunday suit."

"Oh, Jimmie . . ."

"What about your wedding gown?"

"Look at it, Jimmie," I said, holding up a dress that had once been white but now had charcoal-gray stripes across it and was soaking wet.

"Oh, baby, you were so beautiful in that dress. . . ."

Funny how even in the dead of winter the West Virginia sun rises like a watercolor painting over the hills. By the time pink and orange streaks began to glow over the horizon, all we had were a couple of boxes of wet, sooty items. Of everything we'd worked to attain—from our college schoolbooks, to our Sunday best, to the materials we used for teaching— much of it had been destroyed.

We trudged down the stairs carrying boxes and bags, then walked two doors down the street and knocked on the front door. Lights were already on in the kitchen, and when our neighbor let us in, we could smell bacon cooking. Our neighbor motioned us to the bedrooms, where the girls were sleeping. We stood in the doorway and looked at our babies, tears filling our eyes, grateful that they were alive.

"Time to wake up," we whispered as we sat on the bed alongside them. "We're going to White Sulphur."

So after everyone had eaten and bathed, we set out for home. But even after bathing, none of us could get the smell of smoke totally off ourselves. We carried the girls and put them in the back of our 1949 black Chevrolet and set off on the two-hour drive to White Sulphur Springs. They cried the entire way. Not only were we still frightened, but all of our clothes—everything we owned—was just gone! Smoke was in our hair, on our clothes, even on our skin.

I hadn't called Mamá or Daddy before we'd left. So when we pulled up to the house, they were surprised to see us. Once I told them what was going on, Daddy carried the girls, who were still weak and coughing, inside.

"You're going to stay with Mamá and Granddaddy until

the end of the school year," I told them. "Your daddy and I are going to return to Bluefield."

That morning, Daddy called a White man named Mr. Cox who owned a clothing store. Mr. Cox agreed to open his store just for us so we could get the girls clothes. They needed new coats, dresses, leggings, shirts, and pants.

The fire was a real tragedy, but Jimmie, the girls, and I would just have to begin again. Bad things happen, and then life goes on. My brain began to calculate how many days we'd have to work to recover what we had lost. Jimmie and I resolved to do whatever we had to do. The good thing was that we would do it together.

Unfortunately, that wasn't the only tragedy that year. My brother Horace got leukemia after being poisoned during the war. He was taken to the Veterans Affairs hospital in Richmond, but they couldn't save him. My older brother, whom I'd also helped with math when we were in primary school, passed away. I was crushed, even though I knew he'd gone to heaven. Ever since I'd been born, he had been there for me, my big brother. We had been so close.

But there was nothing I could do but keep moving forward.

# CHAPTER 5

"What are you gonna do when you go home for the summer?" Jimmie's sister Margaret asked me.

"Nothing special," I replied.

It was August 1952, and we were in Marion for the wedding of Jimmie's younger sister Pat to her college sweetheart, Walter. We were all just talking and having fun.

"Well, you should come home with us," Margaret said. "Eric will get you a job."

Margaret's husband, Eric, was a Realtor. Since relocating to the Newport News area, they had been doing well. Jimmie was getting tired of teaching, and we were both getting sick of scraping by. We knew there were five military bases in the Newport News–Hampton Roads area: Langley, Fort Eustis, Fort Monroe, the Newport News shipyard, and the National Advisory Committee for Aeronautics, called NACA. The area held so much promise.

"There is some sort of secret government project out here on the Virginia peninsula, and they are looking for Colored women who are mathematicians," Eric told me.

"Really!?"

"They call the women 'computers,' Katherine," he said. "I don't know exactly what they do. But do you think you might be interested?"

"Yes. I want to hear more!"

"Well, I know several women who do that job. I think I can help you get on."

After the fire we needed a fresh start. So we packed up and moved the 358 miles east to the Hampton Roads area, the largest ice-free harbor in the United States and home to some of the nation's most important military installations. With so many military bases there, there were lots of jobs in the area.

Hampton was also the home of Hampton Institute,

a college for Colored students. The institute's most famous graduate was the educator and civil rights leader Booker T. Washington, who would go on to help found the Tuskegee Institute in Alabama. Between the bases and the institute, we thought the area would help us build our life and experience the American dream.

Eric helped us secure a three-bedroom, one-story house in Newsome Park, the segregated neighborhood in Newport News, where they lived. Colored people of all backgrounds lived in Newsome Park: doctors, lawyers, dentists, ministers, teachers, carpenters, brickmasons, plumbers. On our block alone, you could find shipyard workers, a school nurse, a chemistry teacher, and someone who worked for the health department. Newsome Park Elementary was just a two-minute walk away. Though we knew it was inferior to the all-White school, we rested assured with the knowledge that our daughters would be taught by Negro teachers who were both highly educated and well prepared.

Jimmie's sisters Pat and Margaret, and their families, lived right across the street, so from the onset our house was full of life. Because the neighborhood was segregated, it was secure from the dangers that racism posed. But now that we lived in a city for the first time, we exercised an abundance of caution. Because while we understood the rules in White Sulphur, Marion, and Bluefield, in this metropolis we didn't know what types of mistakes with White residents might get the girls in trouble, one of us fired, or our family's life endangered.

To be safe, we taught the girls to stay within a narrow corridor. Don't go downtown. Go to the Colored YWCA but not the all-White youth center. If something happens and you get hurt, go to the Colored hospital, not the White hospital. Don't go to the grocery store by yourself. We taught them to obey the rules and show good manners. Most of all they were to behave respectfully toward White people. Some of our friends taught their children—particularly boys—not even to look at White people at all. Many a Colored man had been lynched over the allegations that he'd looked a White man in the eye or looked at him in an "uppity" way— or, worse, looked that way at a White woman.

In fact, just a few years later, in 1955, a fourteen-year-old Chicago resident named Emmett Till, who was visiting his relatives in Mississippi for the summer, was accused of making verbal and physical advances toward a young White woman, Carolyn Bryant. Her husband and her brother-in-law beat Till, shot him in the head, and threw him into the Tallahatchie River. Bryant didn't admit until she was seventy-four years old that she'd lied. By then it was too late for Emmett or his mother, Mamie—who'd held an open-casket funeral so that all of America could see her son's mutilated corpse—to receive justice in court. By the time the truth came out, Emmett had been dead for fifty-three years and the photographs taken of him in the casket made White America see the brutality it often ignored or denied. Indeed, all of us knew that the rules of segregation were arbitrary and the price for violating them could be vicious. One mistake could ruin not only your life but that of your entire family—and wreak havoc for the entire community.

We began attending Carver Memorial Presbyterian Church with Margaret and Eric. I joined the choir right away. And because I could remember the entire budget in my head, it wasn't long before I became the church treasurer. I also became active with the local chapter of AKA. The sorority tutored, mentored children, did community outreach, and gave out scholarships.

To learn both about the area and about Negro history, our family would sometimes go to Hampton Institute on Sundays after church. We would walk through its tree-lined campus, peek into college classrooms, and admire its magnificent chapel with its vaulted ceiling, grand columns, and multicolored stained glass.

We would also stand together beneath the one-hundred-foot limbs of the famous Emancipation Oak, which reached out to embrace us.

"This is where the first reading of the Emancipation Proclamation took place in the South," I'd tell the girls in a voice I'd lower to a whisper to reflect my reverence of the place. More than one hundred formerly enslaved people had once stood under the tree and learned for the first time that they were free, nearly two years after the law had passed.

"Just imagine what it must have been like for our forebearers who stood under this very tree," I'd say. "During the Civil War they fled the brutality of slavery in search of the promise of safety offered by the Union General Benjamin F. Butler. He had made it known that he would consider people who had escaped to be 'contraband of war' and would protect them from slave patrollers and bounty hunters and would not return them to slavery."

A large encampment of newly freed men and women, called the Grand Contraband Camp, had developed in the area, and these men and women demonstrated a tremendous thirst for education, which was then illegal for Colored people. Many Colored people took the last name Freeman to reflect their newly freed status in the world.

"Then a free Negro woman named Mary Peake began to teach them, even though it was illegal in Virginia to teach Colored people to read," Jimmie would continue, looking deeply into the girls' big brown eyes, wide with wonder. "Mrs. Peake could have been killed for her actions, but she did it anyway. Eventually Brigadier General Samuel Armstrong founded the Institute.

"So, no matter how we are treated in the world, know that our forebearers are people of tremendous bravery and courage."

"You are no better than anyone else," I'd tell them, "but nobody else is better than you."

Shortly after we arrived in Newport News and got settled, Eric helped Jimmie land a job as a painter at the Newport News shipyard. The shipyard was one of the largest ship-building facilities in the world. US Navy battleships, aircraft carriers, ocean liners, oil tankers—all sorts of sea vessels were being built there. Shipyard workers made far more than teachers, so Jimmie was happy to find work there. Before long he was entertaining our daughters by taking them to ship christenings.

The Cold War between the United States and the Soviet Union was in full swing, as the two nations competed in the battle between Communism and democracy.

It was a very scary time.

A series of incidents had taken place in which American citizens had spied for the Soviet Union. To protect our nation's secrets, President Truman had issued an order requiring that all government employees be tested to ensure they were loyal to the United States. This era became known as the Red Scare, and many ordinary citizens were accused of sympathizing with the Communists. Innocent people were fired from their jobs and ostracized by their communities.

The mood had gotten worse in 1949, when the Soviet Union tested an atomic bomb. Suddenly people worried that the Soviets might drop the bomb on us. At that point President Truman ordered the development of the even more powerful hydrogen bomb. From time to time the federal Office of Civil Defense would sound an air-raid siren all around the nation or in local communities so that people could rehearse what to do in the event we were bombed. Schoolchildren were taught to engage in "duck and cover" drills, where they would climb under their desks and protect their heads.

As a result of all this, there was lots of work at the shipyard. The pay was good and—thanks to the pressure of Colored leaders like A. Philip Randolph and the fact that the nation suddenly realized that they needed us—in 1948 President Truman had ordered that discrimination based on race, color, religion, or national origin within the armed forces had to end. With the Soviet threat as great as it was, our nation could not afford to exclude anyone from the workforce. The era required all hands on deck.

After Jimmie started working, I was determined to pursue the job Eric had told me about at NACA. NACA was located at the Langley Aeronautical Laboratory at Langley Field in Hampton. (Today NACA is known as NASA, the National Aeronautics and Space Administration, and Langley Field is known as Langley Air Force Base.) Much of the community worked at Langley, so the more people I met, the more I learned about it.

The Laboratory consisted of eight different departments located in separate buildings. There were wind tunnels, airstrips, and other facilities where researchers tested airplane parts and theories of math and science.

I had heard through the grapevine that a former math teacher named Dorothy Vaughan was running NACA's highly regarded West Area computing unit, which was composed entirely of Colored women. Apparently these women performed mathematical calculations for the engineers at the Lab, who were trying to build state-of-the-art airplanes to keep our nation safe.

Given the threat the Soviet Union posed to us, the work at Langley was very urgent. I'd also heard that Mrs. Vaughan was standing up for the Colored women she supervised, helping them to get better assignments, as well as the promotions and raises they'd previously been denied. Each night I prayed the day would come that I'd be able to join her unit.

One morning after I'd gotten the girls out the door and to school, I removed my head scarf and carefully combed my hair into place, put on my white cotton blouse and a gray sweater and skirt, and then drove myself over to NACA. When I pulled up to the gates, security was especially heavy because of the Red Scare.

Once I'd been questioned about my purpose for visiting and permitted onto the property, I stepped out of my car and walked across the parking lot to the Administration Building. I stood in front of the redbrick facility for a moment, thinking about my long-held dream of becoming a research mathematician. I'd been just a teenager when Dr. Claytor had first told me that I would be a good research mathematician. Now I was thirty-four, a grown woman, married and the mother of three daughters. It had taken all this time and a lot of twists and turns, but I hoped that my dream might be about to come true.

As I stood there, I heard my father's voice in my ears: *You are no better than anybody else, but nobody's better than you.*

I straightened my pearls, brushed the front of my skirt to make sure it was neat, squared my shoulders, and walked up the steps.

Then I pulled open the doors and stepped into a new world. Immediately I was struck by the way men and women were walking by with such a sense of purpose.

I walked into the personnel office, where a White woman sitting behind the front desk looked over the top of her reading glasses at me. I noticed that behind her all of the people in the office seemed to be White.

"How can I help you?" she asked me. I hadn't expected her to be enthusiastic, but I also hadn't thought she'd seem so disinterested.

"I've been told that you are looking for mathematicians," I said.

"You're a mathematician?" she asked, giving my blouse,

my skirt, and my black pumps the once-over. Suddenly, with her inspecting me so, I worried that my stockings might have a run in them.

"Yes, ma'am, I am," I said. "I have been teaching math for the past eight years and am an honors graduate of the West Virginia State College, with bachelor's degrees with high honors in mathematics and French."

"You don't say."

Segregation in the military might no longer have been legal, but the woman exuded an air that indicated she felt superior to me. Later I would learn that the White women who worked at NACA were often the wives of the engineers and got in through nepotism. They didn't feel Colored women belonged, even Black women with degrees.

"Our quota for Colored mathematicians has already been filled this year."

I didn't know whether to believe her or not.

"Do you know when more jobs might open up?"

"Unfortunately, I don't."

"Well, ma'am, I'd like to fill out an application," I said, tightrope-walking between being determined and perhaps seeming impudent. The invisible social line—which, if crossed, might make her think I was sassy—was narrow and was applied arbitrarily.

"You can see if there are some over there on the counter."

There were.

So I sat down, filled the application out, and handed it to the woman.

She scrutinized it, spending a particular amount of time reviewing the courses I'd taken.

"You studied at West Virginia University?" she asked incredulously.

"Yes, ma'am, for one session."

"Well, we will send you a letter if we have any openings."

"Thank you for your time. You'll be seeing me next year."

I wasn't at all confident that she would pass my application on to whomever actually made the hiring decisions.

So my dream was deferred that morning, but I wasn't going to give up. Having patience was part of Negro life. Our leaders and citizen activists pushed local, state, and federal governments and businesses for chances for Colored citizens. We, the public, prepared ourselves and waited for opportunities to open up, and when they did, we walked through the doors.

*Follow new leads and don't give up. Keep trying.* That's what I told myself.

Since it looked like I might not be hired at Langley right away, I applied to become a substitute teacher at the Collis P. Huntington High School. Huntington was a Colored school in the East End neighborhood of Newport News. I returned to the classroom, cherishing the opportunity to share my love of math with young men and women who were eager and determined to learn so that they could assume the place they deserved in American society. By now I had learned that while some students found math easy, many students felt intimidated by it. I'd also come to realize that anyone who doesn't love math hasn't been taught math by someone who felt passionate about it. I loved to meet the challenge.

I rejoiced in teaching young people about linear equations and graphs. We talked about the power of polynomials and solved quadratic equations together. Right triangles and the Pythagorean theorem? It didn't take long for my students to understand them. And my oldest students were swept away into the mysteries of sine, cosine, and tangents.

On the days when I wasn't teaching, I also helped make ends meet as the director of the local United Service Organizations, or USO, assisting members of the military to find jobs and housing.

Even to this day, the USO provides live entertainment, like music and comedy, for members of the armed forces and their families. Since they sacrifice so much, the organization's job is to bring them comfort and laughter. Meeting so many members of military families also gave me the inside scoop on hiring at Langley and helped me make lots of friends.

Before long I learned that NACA had accepted my application but that I wouldn't start work until the following year.

On May 17, 1954, the Supreme Court decided the case of *Brown v. Board of Education of Topeka* by ruling that "in the field of education the doctrine of 'separate but equal' has no place." In the process the court overturned its *Plessy v. Ferguson* decision of 1896. In that proceeding, it had ruled that racially segregated facilities were constitutional as long as they were equal. In another *Brown* decision in 1955, the court ruled that the dismantling of separate school systems must happen with "all deliberate speed."

With the *Brown* decision, Colored people obtained a much-needed boost in our long fight for an equal education—in theory at least. In reality the *Brown* decision didn't go over well among many White people, particularly down South. They became angry and dug in their heels. Though far fewer lynchings took place during the 1950s than occurred earlier in my life, Colored people never knew when the next incident of racial violence would strike. That fear hung over us like the fear of the Russians hovered over everyone else.

During the next several years, one of Virginia's US senators, Harry Byrd, would promote a strategy called the Southern Manifesto, which opposed integrated public schools as a violation of states' rights. More than one hundred congressmen from throughout the Confederacy joined him in encouraging state governments to take actions they called Massive Resistance, using "all lawful means" to resist desegregation. Among many other penalties, Massive Resistance cut off state funds to any public school attempting to integrate, even though integration was officially the law of the land.

The night before my first day of work at NACA, I touched up my navy-blue tweed pleated skirt and jacket and checked my stockings to make sure they didn't have any runs. I woke up the next morning without an alarm clock, excited and a little nervous. I sensed that my life was about to change.

"What secret project do you think the government will have me working on?" I wondered aloud to Jimmie, who lay awake in bed beside me.

Hard at work at NACA.

"I don't know, honey, but I know it will be important."

"I guess I'll have to wait to find out!"

When I arrived at Langley later that morning, I discovered that since I had a bachelor's degree in mathematics, I would be hired as a mathematician. Women whose degrees were in other disciplines were hired to be what were called computers.

I was to report to a branch called West Area Computing and would be on probation for six months.

"Don't come in here in two weeks asking for a transfer," the human resources director told me.

"This is just my first day," I replied, taken aback. "I'm not sure why anyone would do that."

I didn't appreciate her comment, but there was a tightrope I needed to walk. I was really excited about this job—and as a mathematician I would be getting paid three times as much as I'd been paid as a teacher.

My heart beat with excitement as a woman led me over to the Aircraft Loads Building. Then she opened a door and ushered me in.

As I stepped into the room, I witnessed something that

I'd never seen before: a couple of dozen Colored women sitting at desks, typing on Monroe or Friden desktop calculating machines.

What an amazing sight!

I stood there astounded. All of the women were neatly dressed in blouses and jackets and skirts. Back then a room filled with so many professional Colored women was a rare sight. And not one of them was a teacher or a nurse, the professions that were most common for Colored career women. Nor were any of them domestics, the job so many Colored women worked in back then.

Talking with a coworker at Langley.

These were the highly regarded computers I'd been hearing about. The *click, click, click* of their fingers running across the ten-by-ten gray manual keyboards of their calculators resonated throughout the room. Long before the electronic device we now know as a computer came into being, "computer" was the job title given to the women who performed mathematical calculations for Langley's engineers. I knew that the engineers were all men; the computers were all women. Most were White; a smaller number were Colored. I'd learn that all of us were known as computers with skirts.

"Katherine?" A familiar voice from behind me brought me out of my reverie.

I turned around to a smiling woman whose right hand was outstretched—the same woman I'd met back in White Sulphur and whose daughter had often sat on my parents' front porch.

"Dot?"

"Oh, what a small world!" She laughed.

"My goodness! I've heard so many amazing things about you, but I had no idea that the person I've been hearing about was you," I said, recalling our days back in White

Sulphur when the girls were little. "I'm thrilled to be here and am ready to work."

Before long I'd learn that Mrs. Vaughan, as I called her at work, was an honors graduate of Wilberforce University with a degree in math. She had been recruited to Langley in 1943 from Farmville, Virginia, where she had been working as a math teacher. She arrived believing she was accepting a temporary job; however, her work had become so highly respected that not only was she still at Langley years later, but in 1949 she had been promoted to acting head of the group. In 1951 she became one of NACA's first women section heads as well as the base's only Colored manager.

A White woman, Margery Hannah, was the head of West Computing and was Dorothy's boss.

It soon became clear that Dorothy was highly respected by both White people and Colored people. I'd discover that both her work and the work of the West computers was admiringly regarded all over the Lab. And she moved with an authority that I had rarely seen in other Colored women, who were usually required to fill subservient roles. Mrs. Vaughan was accustomed to being in charge.

Each day as they came into our office, I observed that the White male engineers really relied on her to recommend the best computers for each particular job. If she could come from a small town, as I had, to Langley and excel, I was certain that I could too. Dorothy Vaughan was incredibly knowledgeable. She was very impressive; I found her presence inspiring.

The first assignments Mrs. Vaughan gave me involved working with engineers focused on airplane aeronautics. Aeronautics includes the science and practical issues associated with building and flying airplanes. During that era our nation was focused on the goal of supersonic flight, which means that the speed of the airplane is faster than the speed of sound. That's pretty fast. Sound travels at 768 miles per hour. Whenever a plane travels that fast, it creates a shock wave called a sonic boom that sounds like a loud clap of thunder. The base was also creating experimental planes with new shapes that allowed them to fly faster and faster. As the Cold War continued, NACA focused on designing missile warheads. People were also starting to talk about the first humans flying to outer space.

The engineers' job was to come up with the theories and formulas that advanced the nation's aviation know-how; the computers performed and checked calculations to ensure that the engineers' ideas worked. Back then there was a widespread belief that men were just not interested in the small things. They didn't care how you did the work; they would just say, "Give me the answer." It was believed that women would be more attentive to the fine details; men wouldn't have the patience to do that.

If the men's ideas didn't work, the planes wouldn't fly, so the women's work was absolutely essential. Later, I would learn that the women of West Computing could type ten digits at a time into their calculators from memory.

Right away I loved my new job. Suddenly I was using the advanced theorems and skills I'd learned from Dr. Evans and Dr. Claytor. I could immediately see how well they'd prepared me. My class on the math of outer space came in especially handy.

Each morning I'd get up, unfasten the bobby pins that held my pin curls in place, and get dressed. Then I'd awaken the girls and we'd eat breakfast together—usually fruit, cereal, toast, and maybe homemade applesauce. After that we were off to work and school.

My neighbor Eunice Smith, a West computer who lived three blocks over, would pick me up, and she, Alta Brooks (another computer), and I would rush to the office together. The environment at Langley was so stimulating; it was exciting; it challenged every bit of my brain! It was a pleasure to do work that produced results that were so important to the engineers. But even though some of my work is famous today, back then I had no idea that it would one day be important or known the whole world over.

The West computers were extremely committed to our assignments. We did a good job, worked a full day, and fulfilled our responsibilities; that was our mantra. We felt proud to be representing the Colored community in supporting our nation, especially in the face of the threats posed by the Russians.

At NACA, I didn't feel segregation in quite the same oppressive way that I did out in the world. Though there were Colored bathrooms and a Colored section of the cafeteria, I usually ate at my desk. Margery Hannah treated us well, and I spent lots of time working with or for White men and women, which was different from what was happening throughout much of the South. We had a mission and we worked on it. What was important was to do your job.

Of course, at the end of the day, segregation dictated that we went home to separate communities, our children attended separate schools, we worshipped in separate churches—we even shopped for clothes in different places and went to different grocery stores.

But the next day we'd arrive at Langley and come together to do our jobs all over again.

Now, when I first reported to the branch, the men would just hand me work and tell me they needed me to make calculations. Back then women were supposed to stay in their place. Lots of people—both men and women—believed that women were too emotional and that we should stay home and raise the children and leave all the thinking and working up to men. Of course, this belief system was less common among Colored families, since we weren't allowed to have the best jobs. Colored women were very poorly paid, and so were our husbands. Our families needed women's income in order to survive, so as a result most of us worked. Still, in the workforce, women were to stay in their place.

About two weeks into my new job, a man burst into the office, seemingly in a hurry.

"I need two Colored computers," he stated over the din of the typing.

There was a specific reason that he'd come to West Computing as opposed to East Computing, where the White computers worked. The hurdle for White women computers to be hired was lower than it was for Colored women. Indeed, many of them were the engineers' wives. White women could get hired without having a college degree. Colored women were not only required to have a college degree, ideally in math, but they also had to have had a high GPA. In fact, NACA recruited Colored students who had earned honors in math.

Dorothy pointed at me and another woman and said, "Katherine, Erma."

Erma Walker was one of my peers, and boy, she was sharp! Mrs. Vaughan knew that our educational backgrounds and skills matched what that engineer's department was looking for. Later I'd learn that Erma's husband, Cartwright, worked with Jimmie at the shipyard.

We grabbed our purses and lunch bags, then followed the man over to the Maneuver Loads Branch of the Flight Research Division, where we were then assigned to an all-male research team. We were given desks near each other and were each given a calculating machine.

When I sat down, the engineers sitting next to me got up and walked away. I wasn't sure why. Was it because I was Colored? A woman? Something else? There was no way to know for sure, but I found it amusing. Eventually we became good friends.

One of the engineers wanted me to help him analyze some data from a flight test. I was to look through his long calculation sheets and compute an answer for him. That was my job, so I would do it to the best of my ability.

I pulled out my graph paper and my French curves, which would help me draw curves of different radii. But as I double-checked the engineer's math, I saw something unexpected. The calculation didn't look right. I soon discovered that he'd made an error involving a square root.

I thought for a moment about how to approach the situation. It would be unusual for a Colored person to question a White person. I knew that in some situations questioning White people could be quite dangerous. We learned to pick our battles for the greater good and let other things go by the wayside. It was also unusual for a woman to question a man. Back then most women just did what they were told to do. They didn't ask questions or take the task any further.

But if you want to know the answer to something, you have to ask a question. Always remember that there's no such thing as a dumb question except if it goes unasked. Girls and women are capable of doing everything that boys and men are capable of doing. And sometimes we have more imagination than they do.

Knowing this, I took a deep breath before I spoke. "Is it possible you could have a mistake in your formula?"

Now, if the wind tunnels hadn't been running in the background, with their constant whoosh and roar, I might have heard a pin drop in the room.

I'd crossed a social line, and everyone froze. I could

almost hear some of the engineers thinking, *Who is she, a Colored woman, to question a White male engineer?*

The man came over to my desk and looked over my shoulder.

"I could have made a mistake," he said, "but we've been using that formula for years."

"I understand that, sir. I just think that it's inaccurate."

His face began to turn the color of a cherry cough drop.

I was right and he knew it.

Before long it became clear to the men that I'd studied a high level of math known as analytic geometry. Very few men, not to mention women, excelled in that type of math. When I finished that project, I expected to be sent back to West Computing so that Mrs. Vaughn could assign me to the next project, as was the normal protocol.

To my surprise, that never happened. Somehow the engineers "forgot" to return me. Instead they just handed me the next set of calculations—and then the next. Then the next. Then the next. That's when I realized that they needed me, Colored or a woman or not.

And suddenly I found myself a research mathematician!

I was no better than anyone else, but no one was any better than me.

Every time engineers would hand me their equations to evaluate, I would do more than what they'd asked. I'd try to think beyond their equations. To ensure that I'd get the answer right, I needed to understand the thinking behind their choices and decisions. I started asking them "how" and "why."

At first they were surprised. So were Erma and the other Colored computers who occasionally worked with me in that department. Back then men—especially those in prestigious careers—expected that women would not question them.

A couple of the guys looked at me like I should mind my business. Who was I to be doubting them? I was Colored. I was female. They were both men and engineers.

But I was good at what I did, and I wasn't doubting them; I was being curious. Eventually they'd answer.

Then, after a while, in addition to "why," I also started asking "why not" so that I could get to the root of the question.

I didn't allow their side-eyes and annoyed looks to intimidate or stop me. I also would persist even if I thought I was being ignored. If I encountered something I didn't understand, I'd just ask. And I kept asking no matter whose calculations I was evaluating—an engineer's or the head of the entire department.

Having enough information to do my work accurately was essential, so I just ignored the social customs that told me to stay in my place. I would keep asking questions until I was satisfied with the results. Before long the guys began to understand the contribution that I was able to make when I had the answers to the questions that allowed me to think on their level. Quietly the quality of my contribution began to outweigh the arbitrary laws of racial segregation and the dictates that held back my gender.

In this building there was no Colored bathroom, so I just went to the women's room that was there. (Eventually I was someplace at Langley where there was a Colored bathroom, but I refused to use it, and nobody had the nerve to say anything.) I stopped going to the cafeteria altogether. It was too far, so I just ate at my desk. After a while, at lunchtime I began to play bridge with the engineers I worked with.

After my six-month probation, I got a promotion, a raise, and an offer to permanently join the Flight Research Division's Maneuver Loads Branch, whose research included keeping aircraft safe when they were in flight.

Shortly thereafter they assigned me to help solve the mysterious plane crash of a small Piper plane that seemed to have just dropped out the sky on a clear blue day. For months I studied and plotted the data from the plane's flight recorder, noting the plane's altitude, speed, acceleration, and so on, measured during the flight. Eventually the engineers ran a simulation. I analyzed that data as well. My research helped uncover the fact that the plane had flown perpendicularly across the path of a jet that had just gone by. The engineers already knew that swirls of atmospheric wind disturbance, known as wake turbulence, form behind a plane as it flies through the air and can last for as long as half an hour. But what they hadn't known and discovered with the help of my analysis was that the forces associated with wake turbulence can be so great that they can somersault a plane out of the sky. Our research resulted in changes to air-traffic regulations, requiring planes to fly no less than a certain distance apart.

By then the guys were no longer bothered by my questions. They were thrilled that I, too, read *Aviation Week* and was as interested in these problems as they were. Some of the guys eventually became my good friends.

I truly loved going to work every single day—and when you love what you do, it doesn't feel like work!

Enjoying my work!

* • * • * • * • * • * • * * • • * * • •

Between Jimmie's job at the shipyard and my work at NACA, our life in Virginia began to feel so secure that we started thinking about building a new house for our family.

Then, one day in 1954, Jimmie started complaining that the headaches he'd been having were getting worse. At first we just assumed that he needed to rest. But when the headaches didn't stop, we went to see our family doctor, Dr. Scott.

Dr. Scott thought Jimmie had something called undulant fever, caused by the unpasteurized milk and cheese that was commonly consumed at that time. But when his illness didn't subside, the doctor began to think that perhaps a hit on the head that Jimmie had experienced at the shipyard was the cause of his problems. Later the doctors considered that perhaps he'd been poisoned when he'd been stung by several bees while cutting the lawn.

Six months passed before the doctors concluded that the headaches were happening because a part of his brain was growing abnormally. This area had become the size of a lemon or a small orange. They called it a tumor, but it wasn't cancerous. The bad news was that it was located at the back of his head right above his neck. The doctors suspected that he had been born with the tumor and it had suddenly started to grow.

By the time 1955 rolled around, Dr. Scott told us that we needed to see a specialist surgeon. He suggested a White doctor named Dr. Coppola.

"He's the best in the field," Dr. Scott said.

"We can't afford a specialist," I told him.

Desperate, I didn't know what we would do.

"Since you work at NACA, I'll see if he will do the surgery for free."

Dr. Scott talked to Dr. Coppola and told us that Dr. Coppola wanted to visit our family. I knew that we would have to prove that, as Colored people, we were good enough for him to treat Jimmie.

I would serve him tea, and Joylette would play the piano. I talked to the girls about how important it was that they be on their best behavior.

Dr. Coppola came on a Saturday, but we were dressed up in our church clothes. When I opened the door to greet him, he was smaller than I'd expected, smaller than Jimmie.

"Good afternoon, Dr. Coppola," I welcomed him. "Thank you for taking time out of your busy schedule to visit us."

"I'm happy to be here, Mrs. Goble," he said. "Dr. Scott has spoken highly of you."

I ushered him into the living room.

"Dr. Coppola, this is our oldest daughter, Joylette; our middle daughter, Connie; and our youngest, Kathy."

"What a lovely family you have."

"Please, sit down. " I gestured. "Can I get you some tea?"

"Why, yes, that would be nice."

"Joylette, why don't you play the piano for Dr. Coppola while I get him some tea," I said.

As I poured him a cup of tea in our finest china, Joylette played the piano. Then I told the girls to go outside so the adults could talk.

"Jimmie is in the bedroom asleep," I told him.

"I've looked at the reports and would like to examine him if I may," he said.

"Certainly, Doctor."

I took him into our bedroom and turned on the lamp.

Jimmie opened his eyes and I introduced him.

"Nice to meet you, Doctor," he said.

"I hear you're feeling a little under the weather."

"Yes, sir, I am."

Dr. Coppola examined Jimmie, then motioned me out to the living room as Jimmie went back to sleep.

"Well, he definitely needs surgery," he told me.

"Is it bad?"

"The surgery would be exploratory so that we can get a sense of what's going on. This is serious, and it will take about eight hours to complete."

"Oh, goodness!" I managed to say, feeling as if the floor were rocking beneath my feet. "I don't know how we'd afford it."

"Let me worry about that," he said. "You clearly have a beautiful family, and I want to do everything I can to keep it together."

From then on, we worshipped Dr. Coppola.

The operation was scheduled for Monday, the eighteenth of June, but we didn't tell the girls. So when their school let out for the summer the week before, Sister came and took all three of them home to White Sulphur for their vacation.

In the meantime Jimmie's parents came to Newport News to be with us.

On the day of the surgery, Jimmie and I woke up and prayed. After that, we all headed to Riverside Hospital, which was located across the street from a shipyard.

The hospital may have been small, but our doctor was the best. He operated on Jimmie for more than eight hours.

My goodness was I anxious! At first his parents and I chatted. After a while we ran out of things to chat about. We all got quiet. Then we tried to read. The newspaper, a book, the waiting room pamphlet about the power of prayer.

I must have counted every single thing in that hospital. I counted the minutes as they went by on the clock. I counted the number of nurses on shift, the number of people who walked by, the tile squares on the floor, the number of pictures on the wall, the number of chairs. I looked at the clock again, the nurses again, the people, the tiles, the chairs. I did this over and over and over. As I paced through the hospital, I couldn't find enough things to count to help me calm my nerves.

Finally Dr. Coppola emerged.

"The surgery went well," he told me. "He's sleeping."

"Can I see him?"

"Yes, but he's very weak."

A nurse took me to the intensive care ward. Jimmie looked so small and vulnerable as he lay there alone, big bandages on his head.

As soon as I left him, I told his parents and then called Mamá to give her an update.

"How is he?" Mamá asked.

"Dr. Coppola told me it went well, but he hasn't regained consciousness yet."

"Well, is he going to be okay?"

The girls had been listening in on our conversation. Their ears suddenly pricked up and they started asking Mamá questions.

"What do you mean, is he going to be okay? Is something wrong with our daddy?" I heard Joylette's voice in the background.

"Your father's had an operation," Mamá told her.

"An operation?! Why didn't you tell us?" Connie asked.

"We didn't want to worry you."

"We're worried now," Kathy said.

"I want to speak to Mommie," Joylette demanded.

My mother handed her the phone.

"When will he be coming home?"

"Is he going back to work?"

When neither of us could answer, they acted out.

"We want to visit Daddy!"

"You have to come and get us."

"We're gonna thumb our way home."

The next morning the girls were on the first train back to Newport News.

I'd wanted to protect them from life's difficulties, but they wanted to be at home. Truth be told, I was grateful to see them.

The girls, Jimmie's parents, and I were sitting in the kitchen together when Dr. Coppola called.

"He's regaining consciousness. You can come see him."

My hands were shaking as I drove back to the hospital. I walked into the room first, his parents right behind me. The girls had to sit in the waiting room. The man I'd fallen in love with looked so fragile, lying there with the covers off, wearing a diaper. I gave him a kiss and told him I loved him. He stirred. I could tell that he'd heard me.

Then I covered him up and went to get the girls.

"Now, your daddy's head has bandages on it and he's very weak and tired," I told them. "So you'll have to be very quiet."

Then I took them to the room.

"Jimmie, the girls have come to see you. . . ."

His eyes fluttered open and he looked right past me. His face lit up.

"My babies are here!"

The girls started cheering and kissing and loving on him.

"Y'all are too loud, dammit!" he said.

Everyone froze.

Jimmie wasn't a yeller, especially at the girls, and we'd definitely never heard him curse. In that moment we came to understand how much pain he was in.

Over the coming days we would learn that the sounds from the nearby shipyard bothered him. The sounds of his three hospital roommates and their families disturbed him. Dr. Coppola didn't like the fact that Jimmie was sharing a room. It wasn't hygienic enough for someone so sick. So Dr. Coppola had him transferred to Mary Immaculate, a Catholic hospital, in order to get him into a private room.

* * . * . * * . * . * *. * * . *

The next several months were very difficult for all of us. At first Jimmie returned to Newsome Park to recuperate. Once the bandages finally came off, he had a scar that looked like a zipper that ran from the back of his head to the bottom of his neck. His mobility had been affected and he was in pain, but he could still get around with a cane. He needed quiet a lot. My friend Erma from work basically adopted our girls. She would come to get them and keep them occupied and buy them little extras that we couldn't afford now that Jimmie was no longer working.

It was wonderful to have Jimmie home. In time, he gained the strength to cook dinner sometimes, one of his favorite pastimes. But he would have setbacks. That fall he went back to the hospital for a week or two of follow-up testing.

Frustrated with the lack of progress, his mother called him home to Marion to see the local doctor. That doctor delivered the devastating news that the tumor had started to grow back.

One day the doctors told Jimmie and me that he was dying. I would have dropped to my knees and dissolved into a puddle, except I didn't want to completely lose my composure in front of him. I was going to suffer the loss of the love of my life and our girls' father, but he would have to say goodbye to all of us. No amount of time is enough to prepare. Though we were grateful to the doctor for the advance warning, learning that Jimmie was going to pass away was a devastating blow to both of us.

Jimmie had been given several months to live, so we thought it would be smart to give ourselves a few months to grieve. We held hands constantly, even when he was resting, our fingers rarely leaving the other's. He would tell me that I

Our previous Christmas together with dear Jimmie.

was beautiful and hold my hand against his heart. When he slept, I would kiss his forehead and eyelids delicately.

We also took care of practical matters. When he was up to it, we would talk about the future. How I would provide for myself and the girls in his absence. That they would continue to play tennis, piano, and violin. Our determination that our daughters would attend college. The new home we'd been planning. How I should take care of the girls and be happy.

It was close to Thanksgiving before we told the girls. Of course, they were crushed and wanted to spend every waking moment with him. They would come to the hospital after school, and even though Connie and Kathy were too young for visiting hours, the nurses would let them in. By mid-December, the doctors told us he wouldn't live until the end of the week.

Jimmie passed away on Thursday, December 20, 1956, about eighteen months after the surgery, and one week before Joylette's birthday.

It was early evening when the angels took him home. Mamá told the girls, and I headed home to them, rushing to comfort them yet dreading what I knew was to come.

"Why aren't you crying?" I asked when I arrived.

Apparently someone had told them not to cry.

"Y'all can cry," I told them. "Come here and cry."

We all hugged one another, and the girls just melted into me and sobbed. Somehow I managed to keep it together. I didn't want to scare them with the depth of my grief, so I saved my tears for after they went to sleep, when Mamá and Daddy could comfort me. Of course, Jimmie's parents and family came to be with us as well.

By noon the next day, a floral arrangement from the school was delivered to our door along with twelve hundred dollars that the school had collected to help with funeral costs. To give you a sense of how much that was, it's almost thirteen thousand dollars in today's money. It was just a stunning amount that people had shared with us overnight. Our neighbors cooked for us, and the house became fragrant with the comforting scents of bacon, biscuits in the oven, fried chicken, and candied yams. Baskets of food began to arrive from the shipyard.

The funeral took place that Sunday at Carver Memorial. The fact that we woke up to rain seemed to fit how all of us felt.

*Even God is crying*, I thought.

Jimmie's homegoing service was huge. He was the first of his siblings to pass away. His parents and siblings attended along with spouses and many of their children. People from church, the girls' school, the USO, and the community came. So did the women from West Computing and some of the White men I worked with at the base. There were a lot of tears.

In the days that followed, the girls and I did a lot of crying together. One day after I broke down in Daddy's arms, he shared with me that he had seen this coming.

"What do you mean?" I asked him, astounded.

"As soon as I met him, I saw early death."

My jaw dropped open.

"That's why I didn't want you to marry him," he continued.

"And I was so angry with you. How did you know?" I asked desperately.

"I saw it in his eyes, Katherine."

I wondered what Daddy had seen that I hadn't been able to see. But it was good to know what Daddy had been feeling. All this time I'd harbored the little niggling thought that he hadn't trusted me. I should have known that Daddy's thinking ran deeper than that.

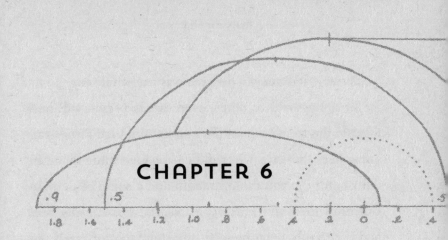

# CHAPTER 6

One. Foot. In. Front. Of. The. Other. Sometimes that's all you can do to get through the day, hour, or even the minute. And each time you do that, it is a triumph. Because there's nothing anyone can tell you to prepare you for life after your husband and first love has passed away. After your daughters' father has passed away. Indeed, in the days after Jimmie's death, I wasn't even thinking of myself. Joylette, Connie, and Kathy were heartbroken. Jimmie and I had known this was coming, so we'd had a little more time to prepare. Now there was no time to focus on myself. It took everything I had to help the girls get through. Sometimes our minutes seemed endless. For weeks we cried freely. Our grief was overwhelming.

At some point or other, every single person will have to scale the rough side of life's mountain. God gives us no guarantees that our road will be easy. Over time that difficulty can help you build strength and a sense of purpose. But until then you hurt. As a Colored woman, my neck had constantly been beneath the stony foot of racial segregation, so collapsing under the weight of a bad twist of fate was a luxury I did not have. Because our parents had built us up from the inside to know that no matter what life threw at you, someone would have your back, I knew I would endure. As long as you have love, you can make it.

Fortunately, we got a lot of love. My family; Jimmie's family; our church family; our neighbors; his friends from the shipyard and mine from NACA; my AKA sorority sisters, Jimmie's friends from his fraternity, Alpha Phi Alpha Fraternity, Inc.; people from the girls' school—the entire community wrapped their arms around us. Folks kept us company, gave us someone to talk to, brought us meals, did our grocery shopping, took care of our yard, helped us to keep the house clean. For weeks people covered us with love.

Two weeks after the funeral, the holiday break came to an end. It was time for me to return to work and the girls to go back to school. As heavy as our hearts were, life goes on. The girls were twelve, thirteen, and sixteen years old by now, old enough to be responsible with their own school-work and helping around the house.

"I need you to have my clothes ironed and ready for me in the morning and dinner fixed when I come home at night," I told our daughters.

This was now our life.

So in early January of 1957, I drove the girls to school and took them to the office of the principal, Mr. Hines.

"Thank you very much for all the ways you have supported us," I told him. "You and the staff have been wonderful!"

"Oh my goodness, Mrs. Goble, it's the least we can do."

"You have supported our family through Jimmie's illness and death," I said. "But we have to move on with our lives. The girls must get ready for college now, and I have to go back to work."

"Yes, ma'am . . ."

"I expect them to do well in their classes. They won't give you any trouble."

Then I kissed my girls goodbye, told them to get to class, and got into the car and drove to Langley.

As a practical matter, at thirty-eight I now had to raise our daughters on my own. I would have to become our breadwinner and carry all of the financial weight. Fortunately, I knew that the way we had raised them, there were very few issues that they could not handle. So I would go to work in the morning, come home in the afternoon to check on the girls, and then go back to work in the evening. Many times, I put in fourteen-to-sixteen-hour days in order to get the job done.

Initially NACA had started space exploration as a "black," or secret, project. The agency envisioned itself developing the technology to launch weather satellites, probes we could send to the moon, and satellites that could warn us if a missile was coming.

But on October 4, 1957, the Russians launched a satellite into orbit, the world's first to reach outer space, the part of space that sits beyond the Earth's atmosphere and in which all of the suns, moons, planets, galaxies, and other celestial bodies exist. The satellite was called *Sputnik*, which means "fellow traveler." *Sputnik* was unmanned, which means that no astronaut rode in it. However, it proved that America was not ahead of Russia in space technology, as we'd previously believed. With the Cold War going on, Americans began to fear for their safety. What if the Russians used *Sputnik* to spy on us? What if they used it to launch a nuclear warhead and drop a bomb on us? And speaking of "traveler," what other weapons did the Russians possess that might be able to voyage here to the US?

The list of scary scenarios was endless.

Then, as if the *Sputnik* satellite wasn't frightening enough, just one month later the Russians launched *Sputnik 2*, which carried a dog as a passenger.

People were panicked. The United States had to protect itself.

I didn't know it then, but the *Sputnik* satellites would change my life forever.

One month later, as a countermeasure, the United

States tried to send up its first test vehicle, named *Vanguard*. In theory the *Vanguard* should have made it into orbit. In reality it lifted just three feet off the launch pad before it burst into flames.

What a humiliating defeat!

With *Sputnik 2*, the Russians had put a satellite into orbit that weighed eleven hundred pounds. We couldn't get a three-pound satellite off the ground.

America had to do better.

But how?

We realized that for our country to advance to the next level, we would have to join together to educate ourselves and one another. Up until that point, no one had written a textbook about space. Suddenly we realized that in order to lead our nation forward and keep the world safe, we would have to write our own.

So early in 1958, three divisions of NACA, including the Flight Research Division I'd been a part of, came together to educate one another about what we each knew. Perhaps each division possessed information that would be helpful to the others. We shared what we knew about the mechanics of how objects operate in space, flight trajectories and how to guide flying objects, propulsion, heating and materials, and the environment in space.

A number of the engineers I'd been working with gave a series of lectures, as everyone educated everybody else. Each day we worked with what we knew, starting with geometry and moving forward from there. Some mathematical calculations I had performed became part of the document we created, *Notes on Space Technology*. It was a joy to contribute to the literature on space.

But my good news was tempered by a bittersweet reality. On May 5, 1958, racial segregation was officially ended at Langley. Though this would normally be cause for celebration, West Computing became a casualty of progress, as the department was dissolved. Though Dorothy Vaughan would continue her career at Langley, her job as the manager of West Computing was over.

On July 29, 1958, President Eisenhower signed the National Aeronautics and Space Act into law. Just two months later, on October 1, NACA was absorbed into the new agency that the Space Act had formed, the National Aeronautics and Space Administration, or NASA. That's when the Space Race began to escalate. Plans to send a man into space, a manned flight to the moon, weather satellites, and other very ambitious objectives, like understanding zero-gravity weightlessness, would all be part of NASA's work.

I found myself right in the thick of the action. I loved understanding the moon and the stars and the stories we were telling about what was possible for humanity. I found working with such interesting and intelligent people tremendously energizing. Still, I was always aware that even with as much education as the engineers had, my father, with his sixth-grade formal education, was equally intelligent.

By that point, my race and my gender seemed to matter far less than they had when I'd first been hired. Of course, my lighter skin color, which some White people saw as less threatening and more like them, played a role in that. I took pride in my work—plus I had been raised and educated to value excellence—so the quality of everything I produced was always top-notch. Everything I worked on, every calculation I performed, was accurate to the extent of my ability.

In fact, among the things that I enjoyed most about math was that if I gave someone an answer last year, it remained the same today.

We were putting our heads together to solve some of the world's most difficult problems. With the nation's security on the line, it was imperative that the most capable people be in the room no matter who they were. Because I had been working with that set of guys, I became part of the group. Despite President Truman's 1948 order, barriers still existed that prevented Colored people and women from participating equally—and still do.

With my coworkers at NASA. I'm in the second row, second from the left.

It also helped that I'd already been absorbed into the Space Task Group team, NASA's first official effort to conquer space. Anyone who didn't like it just had to go along with it.

And that's how I became one of the fortunate handful of people with the honor of creating the foundations for America's path into space.

I will never forget the day when all the engineers—in other words, all the guys—were about to go to a briefing to discuss, well, I didn't know exactly what since I had never been invited. (Whether it was because I was Colored or a woman—or both—I never knew.) That didn't make a lot of sense to me. Since I would be doing the calculations on whatever ideas they discussed, I thought that I should be in the meeting too. By then I was already working on top-secret projects. But because I didn't attend the meetings, I never really knew exactly what was happening. This crippled my ability to do my best work.

Not only was the situation not very smart, but it wasn't the best thing for our nation. So, that day, as the engineers gathered their papers and prepared to go to the meeting, I decided to ask them, "Can I go too?"

Well, after the words came out of my mouth, everyone froze like Popsicles.

"The girls don't go," came the response.

"Why not?"

"They just can't."

"Is there a law against it?" I asked.

Everyone knew there wasn't a law. At the root of it, I was questioning the social convention. The guys looked at one another sheepishly. Whatever they decided in the meeting would be handed over to me to calculate anyhow. I was an essential member of the team, and everyone knew it.

"No," came the response. "There isn't a law."

"Well, I'm the one who will do the work you'll discuss. I need to understand all of what's going on. I belong there."

"Let her go," said my boss.

So beginning in 1958, I attended the briefings right along with all the guys. Being in the room helped me understand more about the geometry of the space program as well as the mapping between locations that I was constantly asked to calculate. It was an easy transition.

Being able to fully participate on the team helped me do

a better job. It also allowed me to demonstrate my natural curiosity. I always wanted to try to get to the root of each question.

Someone would share an idea that I'd have to calculate. But that wasn't all of the information I'd need.

"What happens next?" I would ask.

My questions helped me understand better. They also helped the engineers understand better. Questions helped me to do an even better job and become an even more highly valued member of the team. I didn't do anything alone; we did it together.

As exciting as my workdays were, I didn't bring my work home with me. I didn't discuss what I did. The girls just knew it was math and that I was working on the space program.

Instead I tried to provide them with a good life and make up for the loss of their dad. Just as my father had been determined to send his children to college even though he had never been, I was determined that my girls would go too.

To give us a fresh start in a place without all the sad

memories, I continued with the plan Jimmie and I had had to build a one-story ranch-style brick home in a neighborhood of Colored professionals in Hampton. For weeks Daddy oversaw the project while the house builders poured the concrete. Once the house was built, Connie planted several crape myrtle bushes out front.

We moved into our new house on Mimosa Crescent during the summer of 1958. I encouraged the girls to pick out the colors they wanted for their rooms. As the oldest, Joylette would get her own room, though she would be heading off to college soon. She selected a shade of salmon. Connie and Kathy would share their room; they chose beige. I picked aqua for my bedroom, which I would now sleep in alone. Like the sky blue on our porch roof in White Sulphur, it was a color that gave me hope.

Jimmie and I hadn't imagined that he would never live in the home we were planning; however the new house gave the girls and me a chance to heal without everything in Newsome Park being a reminder of what we'd lost. Family and friends rallied around us. Though we now lived in a city much larger than White Sulphur Springs or Marion or Bluefield, we felt everyone's small-town love, care, and concern. Our hearts mended and we began to move on.

The girls studied hard.

"Do your best," I'd tell them. "But figure out what you like to do. If you like something, you will do your best."

They all did well in math. Eventually, Joylette even became a mathematician.

The girls made lots of friends at school and in our church's youth choir. They also played tennis and took piano lessons. During the evenings and on weekends, we sewed together. I would stitch them beautiful dresses, but I also taught them to sew. I held house parties and card parties to help keep them entertained at home and so they would be safe from segregation's sting as well as its perils. We cheered Althea Gibson on as she integrated professional tennis (and, later, golf) and won Wimbledon in England and the French Open. Little did I know that Joylette would one day meet Althea as well as Arthur Ashe, who integrated men's tennis, when they played in the American Tennis Association championships at Hampton Institute.

Of course, being Colored, my daughters were excluded

from the social activities of White society, including those in which women would prepare their daughters for the world of courting and marriage. White people in high society wanted their daughters to marry men of their same social standing or higher. Though Colored women's place in the pecking order of American society was lower than that of White women, we had fought to obtain an education and to become middle class, and we aspired for our daughters to marry like-minded men.

In 1955, while Jimmie had been so sick, a woman named Rosa Parks had been arrested in Montgomery, Alabama, for refusing to give up her seat on a bus to a White person, violating the city's racial segregation laws. Black people had boycotted the city bus system there for an entire year, and the Supreme Court had ruled that segregation on public buses was unconstitutional, forcing the city to change its laws. I felt hopeful that the nation was changing and that our daughters would have a better future.

But I was a mathematician (and a widow), so my girls didn't have the social standing of White people or of the children of the Colored doctors, lawyers, and ministers. So

I joined together with several of the women from church and the community to form an organization we called the Junior League. Its purpose was to prepare our young ladies for a world we envisioned that they would eventually enter, including a more integrated America. They would become debutantes, where they would come out to society their senior year in high school as eligible to date and eventually marry. (Back then we assumed that almost everyone would get married.)

We taught the girls what were then called the social graces—things like how to set a table, how to behave in social settings, how to dress for the formal events that we aspired for them to attend, and so on. For their safety, we taught them not to go anywhere or get into a car with a male unchaperoned—not that there was anywhere, really, for them to go aside from the house parties thrown by friends, especially with this being the segregated South. I chuckle at it now, but we also warned them against wearing black, a color we associated with being mature, with being grown.

From time to time I'd talk to the girls about space. We'd talk about the full moon, half-moon, and quarter-moon. I'd teach them how to find the planets in the sky, especially Mercury, Venus, and Mars, which are closest. I'd show them how to find some of the constellations: the Big and Little Dippers, Orion's belt, and others. Sometimes I'd take them outside and point out a satellite to them.

Other than that, I left my work at Langley, and our house became a home.

Meanwhile in Washington, President Eisenhower had signed the Civil Rights Act of 1957. It established a permanent federal office to support civil rights and help ensure that everyone could vote. However, the overwhelming majority of White Southern citizens, as well as leaders of all stripes—from political, to religious, to civic—continued to resist the Supreme Court's *Brown* decision. In Little Rock, Arkansas, the Black community, led by newspaper publisher and NAACP chapter head Daisy Bates, was fighting to desegregate. But the opposition was so great that President Eisenhower sent the 101st Airborne Division of the US Army to guarantee that a group of children, who had become known as the Little Rock Nine, had safe passage as they tried to integrate Little Rock Central

High School. Between the troops in military gear who were there to protect them from the White adults, and the young White people who were spitting upon and threatening them, the Colored children walked into what must have felt like a war zone.

The fight over integration in our area was furious as well. The federal courts ordered public schools in Newport News and Norfolk to integrate. Though the entire country was witnessing the military enforcing integration in Little Rock, state and local authorities in Virginia pushed back nevertheless. An all-White Pupil Placement Board responsible for assigning individual students to schools was created. Needless to say, they continued to assign White students to all-White schools and Colored students to Colored schools, which had inferior facilities though often superior teachers. Schools that considered integrating would have their funds cut off.

Now, maintaining segregation created some ridiculous situations. For example, in order to keep Colored people out of Virginia's all-White universities, the state would award Colored students grant money to go to schools in other states. Sister and Charlie were perfect examples. During the summers after they graduated from college, both attended graduate school elsewhere. Eventually Sister got her master's degree from Columbia University and Charlie got his at New York University, both in New York City—paid for by their resident states, West Virginia and North Carolina, respectively, where each was working. It's just one way that so many Colored educators ended up better trained than their White counterparts.

All throughout the South, courageous Colored lawyers and activists supported by organizations like the NAACP continued to risk their lives to fight for equality. This was very dangerous work. White people opposed to integration were known to spit, sic dogs on people, throw rocks at them, hurl bricks or fire bullets through living room windows, burn down houses with people in them, and even shoot or lynch people—yet no one in their families or communities would tell on the perpetrators. Every Sunday morning, our congregation would pray for the safety of our leaders, and for these courageous children and their families engaging in sit-ins and other direct forms of protest.

During the fall of 1958, our family celebrated as Joylette

became a first-year student at Hampton Institute, continuing both the Coleman and Goble families' respective legacies of doing whatever it took to send our children to college, and demonstrating her determination to better herself despite the devastating loss of her dad. I felt proud knowing that she, too, planned to major in math and imagined herself working at NASA.

That same month the all-White authorities who ran the government of Norfolk delayed the start of public school in an effort to resist the court's mandate that the city integrate. As the White authorities fought to keep our children out of their schools, the Colored community, churches, and educators came together to keep our children learning. When the schools finally opened several weeks later, the state's governor, James Lindsay Almond Jr., ordered them closed again. Before long a group of White families sued the state because Colored children weren't the only ones being hurt by the shutdown; children in all-White schools were being harmed as well. Other White parents began petitions and letter-writing campaigns.

In January 1959, the Virginia Supreme Court of Appeals

ordered that Norfolk's schools be reopened, though it also stated that it believed that the *Brown* decision violated states' rights. The mayor of Norfolk resisted, even though much of the school year had been lost by then and children's education undermined. Finally a judicial panel ordered the schools open again. Five years passed between the *Brown* decision and the time when the first, very courageous Colored children successfully integrated any Virginia public school. But because the danger was so grave, hardly any Negro students dared to cross the color line.

As much as I believed that Negro people should have an equal opportunity to participate in American society, there were realities to deal with. Among them: Who was going to protect our children at a White school where they weren't welcome? The last thing I wanted was to place my daughters in harm's way by integrating Newport News's schools. And aside from a better building, what would be in it for them? It was a well-known fact in the Colored community that Negro teachers were more highly trained. On top of that, the city offered to pay three hundred dollars per child for Connie and Kathy to continue to attend the Colored high school in

Newport News. That was fine with me and it was fine with them. Kathy was a junior and Connie was a senior, and they wanted to graduate with their friends. Plus their high school had the only orchestra in the local high schools, Black or White.

"As long as you can find a way to school, you can keep going to Carver High School in Newport News," I told them.

"We're gonna find a ride, Mommie," they told me.

Their teachers went out of their way to pick them up each morning in order to drive them to school.

As much as I valued education and was experiencing the benefits of mine, I didn't want my girls' lives to be endangered. To keep them safe, I watched who they made friends with and set rules that they could only travel around the area within a very narrow zone—mostly on our street or on Marshall Avenue, a main street through the Colored section of Newport News.

Although I prayed and persevered and tried my best not to worry, the reality was that once I drove outside the gates at Langley, neither my life nor the lives of my children were safe. That reality became even more clear in 1960, when young Negroes—first in Greensboro, North Carolina, and then throughout the South—began engaging in nonviolent sit-ins at Whites-only lunch counters both to desegregate public space and to gain support for the civil rights movement by exposing the violence of the Jim Crow laws that legalized segregation.

Now that she was in college at Hampton Institute, I worried about Joylette's involvement. Once, she told me that she wanted to participate in a sit-in at the lunch counter of the Woolworth's, a retail department store chain, on Main Street in Hampton.

"I don't want you to participate, Joylette," I told her. "If you get arrested, you'll have a record and won't be able to work at NASA."

Many of my adult friends felt conflicted—both wanting greater freedom for their children and fearing for their safety as they fought to integrate American society.

Just as many other young people ignore some of their parents' advice, Joylette participated anyhow, though she didn't tell me everything until later. One day, we sat at the

kitchen table as she explained how she had attended a training to prepare herself to practice nonviolence even if she
was attacked, as had happened during many other protests.
My heart was in my throat as she described the sit-in itself.

"I was sitting at the lunch counter looking in the mirror in
front of me at the White people behind me, wondering what
they might do to me," she told me. "I was scared to death."

Fortunately, the sit-in ended without anything happening to her.

With all of the departments of NASA moving in the same
direction, in August of 1959, NASA finally launched a satellite that worked in every respect. Six months later the agency
launched a different rocket to explore the space between
Earth and Venus. One month after that, our nation's first
weather satellite went up. It was an era of firsts.

In the meantime, I was working on calculations for
two different possible orbits for the first manned trip to
the moon. Of course, those calculations would have to be
perfect, because it was one thing to send a man into outer
space, but it was another thing to bring him home safely

again. (Back then all astronauts were men; we have women astronauts now.)

The astronauts were very brave, and many were already war heroes or had taken tremendous risks to push the boundaries of knowledge, and we committed ourselves to ensuring that they would return home to their wives, children, and other loved ones in one piece. Sometimes we would see the astronauts walking around the base. We were amazed by them. Once, we got to meet them and learned that *they* were in awe of *us*! Certainly, they knew that their lives were in our hands.

We pored over our calculations for weeks on end. Our days were long, but I loved working with smart people, and people respected my answers because my answers were always correct.

I knew from my college studies that the rocket's trajectory into space would be in the shape of a parabola, a plane curve that is identical on both sides and shaped roughly like the letter U. (In this case, our parabola would look like an upside-down U.) The fact that both sides are identical made it fairly easy for me to predict where the capsule would be at any particular point in time. To retrieve the astronaut safely, we had to make sure that we understood the exact place and time that space capsule would touch down.

For an orbiting object to land at a specific location on Earth at a specific time, it has to be navigated to a precise point in outer space. That point, called the azimuth, is where the process of bringing the spacecraft down to the landing point would begin. One of my jobs was to calculate the azimuth. I had to consider factors such as when the rocket would have to fire, when they would need to launch the spacecraft away from the rocket, the weight of the space capsule with all the equipment and astronaut in it, the rocket's speed, the rotation of the Earth, and many other indispensable pieces of data. After the engineers worked out their formulas, I would plug all of the missing numbers into their equations to see if their formulas worked mathematically. One wrong formula on their part—or one inaccurate piece of data provided to me or one mistaken calculation by me—could mean a disaster for the astronaut and a tragedy for his family. The calculations had to be accurate out to many, many decimal places.

In 1960 one of my peers, engineer Ted Skopinski, and I published a report that determined the azimuth angle—the angle of the capsule's velocity—at the precise moment when the astronaut flying the capsule would turn its rockets off. At that point, the force of gravity would take over and the capsule would free-fall down to the landing point. I calculated two sample orbits—one with a rocket launching from the east, and the other from the west. When this report was published, it was the first time that a woman in our Flight Research Division received credit as an author of a research report. Prior to that, the women computers would perform all sorts of computations included in agency reports, but only the men's names would be put on the cover. The women did their share of the work, but they weren't given any credit. Having my name on the cover of this report was a really big deal and opened the door to other women being acknowledged for their work.

During this time we began considering a plan to send astronaut Alan B. Shepard Jr. into the atmosphere. Of course, we also had to figure out how to bring him down and land him in a specific place so that the navy could retrieve both him and the capsule out of the ocean.

"Let me do those computations," I said. "You tell me where you want the capsule to land, and I'll work the formula backward and tell you where to take off."

Then I computed his trajectory. That was my forte.

From then on, whenever a flight trajectory was needed, the engineers from the other divisions would send word to our branch, and I would work all the calculations by hand.

By that time NASA was starting to use electronic computers made by International Business Machines, or IBM. At first people didn't have all that much confidence in the IBM computer. In addition to the periodic glitches and blackouts, there were times when electronic computers would spit out answers so unexpected that it wasn't clear if the machines were up to snuff. The engineers would ask me to double-check the electronic computer's accuracy. I'd do the math manually. In the beginning the IBM wasn't always correct.

In those days the engineers accepted whatever answer I gave them, above the computer. Over time computers became increasingly accurate—and they were certainly a lot faster than a human being. In fact, some of my calculations from the azimuth angle report had been programmed into it, allowing them to be performed more quickly. Some of the other "computers in skirts" lost their jobs to the electronic machine. (In fact, the machines became so fast that after we reached a point where we knew we could trust them, I would give some of my own problems to the computers.)

At work on my computer.

Fortunately, as the smartest human computer out of all of us, Dorothy Vaughan had been thinking ahead. Over the years that electronic computers had been coming online, she had trained both herself and the Colored women of West Computing she supervised in how to run the IBM machines. The women's willingness to learn new skills and reinvent themselves helped many of them save their jobs.

But despite all our progress, the US space program wasn't moving fast enough. On April 12, 1961, the first Russian astronaut flew into outer space. He traveled all the way around the Earth—a total of twenty-four thousand miles. During that voyage, he experienced eighty-nine minutes of weightlessness.

Finally, a few weeks later, early in May of 1961, we prepared to launch the Mercury-Redstone spacecraft, named *Freedom 7*, with astronaut Alan Shepard Jr. inside it.

I will never forget that Friday morning.

The skies were clear and turquoise blue as the *Freedom 7* sat atop Launch Pad 5 at Cape Canaveral Air Force Station in Florida. Standing tall and proud on the launch pad was the slender white rocket with a black cone and the words

REACHING FOR THE MOON

"United States" written in red paint down its side.

Everyone involved was very nervous, hoping that everything we'd done was right.

Finally, at 9:34 a.m., everyone's hard work paid off. The *Freedom 7* successfully lifted off from the launch pad.

"What a beautiful view," Shepherd told the command center as he looked out the tiny porthole of his capsule, flying high enough to see the Earth's curve.

That day the *Freedom 7* traveled for a total of 15:02 minutes and 302 miles at an altitude of 115 miles high in the sky. It was the first time that the United States had ever put a man in space, but compared to the Soviet Union, we were still far behind.

One day a few years earlier, brilliant pink blossoms bloomed on the crape myrtle that Connie had planted in our yard. And just when I thought I'd never love again, God dropped a wonderful man right into my lap.

I was minding my business one Sunday morning when our pastor introduced a new member of our church.

"He's single, ladies," our pastor said.

The gentleman was tall and handsome, but I didn't pay him any mind. I was both a widow and a mother. I was also forty years old—practically a spinster by that era's standards.

But at a church cookout this new gentleman, James Johnson, seemed to take a liking to me. Later, I learned that our pastor had told him, "I have a young widow with three daughters that I'd like you to meet."

Love came as quite a surprise.

James, who went by the name Jim, was a military man.

Back when he was in high school, he lied about his age in order to get into the navy. Later he attended Hampton Institute, but before graduation and while in their ROTC program, he was drafted and served as an army artillery officer for four years during the Korean War. After the war ended, he obtained one of the few good jobs available to Negro men of that era—that of a mail carrier. He then went on to complete his degree, attend the National War College, become a lieutenant colonel in the army reserves, and volunteer on Hampton's ROTC staff for fifty years.

Along the way Jim joined the church choir. He sang bass, as my husband Jimmie had. But having the same name and

singing voice was where the similarities ended. Their personalities were as different as night and day. While Jimmie
had been very social and outgoing, Jim was a bit bashful, a
loner, very quiet, and liked to read.

Before long Jim and I started going to dances and dinner parties together. He began sitting with the girls and me

Jim and I on our way to a formal ROTC event.

at church. Then he proposed. It wasn't like the scene in the movie *Hidden Figures*, where the girls were involved. That was fictionalized for Hollywood. But the girls did know and like him. He was very good to us and was at all times extremely supportive of me.

In August 1959, Jim and I got married. I took his name and became Katherine Johnson.

In November of 1960, at only forty-three years old, John F. Kennedy became the youngest man elected president. I will never forget how in his inaugural speech on January 20, 1961, he called on Americans to come together to end poverty and win the Cold War. His timeless words—"Ask not what your country can do for you; ask what you can do for your country"—will echo in my ears forever.

That March, the president issued an executive order prohibiting discrimination in the federal government on the basis of race, religion, or national origin. It would move Negroes one more important step forward toward legal equality, though many of the realities of life would take decades to change.

President Kennedy also wanted to know what needed to happen for the United States to surpass the Soviet Union in space. That May he stood before Congress and called for the United States to commit to, within the decade, "landing a man on the moon and returning him safely to Earth." This led to the establishment of the Apollo space program, and everyone's efforts shifted, since now our entire nation would be reaching for the moon.

But landing a man on the moon raised a tremendous number of questions.

Some members of the public wondered if the moon was made of Swiss cheese. Scientists wondered if its surface was rock or whether it was covered with dust. And if dust-covered, how deep was that coating? So deep that a spacecraft landing upon its surface might sink into it and even disappear? What was the moon's atmosphere like? Could men survive outside of the space capsule? How would astronauts refuel the spaceship for the voyage home?

Many questions remained to be answered—and I was among those asking them.

We knew that the crew would need a spacecraft able to

blast off from Earth, overcome gravity, enter outer space, travel to the moon, refuel, and return. Our goal was to be able to do that on February 20, 1962.

Our group computed the launch windows. Everybody was concerned about getting the astronauts to the moon, but we were worrying about them getting back. Because if you miss your plane, you may not get another flight for six hours. But if an astronaut who had landed on the moon missed his connection with the orbiting vehicle, he was done for. There was no way he could get back to planet Earth ever again. So we did calculations on how much error the astronauts could allow—determining, for instance, that an astronaut could miss the vehicle by no more than x number of degrees, or no more than y speed per second.

I worked night and day to get it right, often with one of my colleagues, engineer Al Hamer, whom I collaborated with on several reports. We considered all sorts of "what if" scenarios. Our goal was to make the trip to the moon less risky than going for a drive in a Corvette on a Sunday afternoon.

On February 20, 1962, astronaut John Glenn walked out to the *Friendship* 7 rocket we hoped would place the first American in orbit.

Glenn was a marine fighter pilot who had flown fifty-nine combat missions in the South Pacific during World War II. In 1957, he had made the first supersonic flight across the entire United States, flying from Los Angeles to New York in three hours and twenty-three minutes. He was handsome, blond, and charismatic, and everyone on the base knew who he was and what he was training to do. As I understood it, off the base he was also very popular—at the grocery store, church, ball games, and the like—in the White part of the community. No matter what the new laws stated, neighborhoods remained racially segregated. Many have stayed that way.

Glenn's training was very rigorous, including his physical fitness. For example, in addition to understanding the spacecraft's automatic control panel, he was taught how to manually control the capsule in the event that the automatic controls failed. He trained in how to operate under conditions of what we then called weightlessness, or zero gravity—when a person floats around in the air. That condition takes place between two hundred and two hundred and fifty miles above Earth's surface. (Today we call it microgravity, since gravity never actually goes away.) Glenn was trained what to do if the capsule started rocking from side to side, or spinning in circles, or pitching forward and backward—or all of these at the same time—as it hurtled through space at seventeen thousand miles per hour. He practiced survival training in the sea and on land. Every possible scenario anyone could think of was covered. And while he trained, we theorized, questioned, and calculated.

A feat like this involved tremendous complexity. The agency had constructed a way to communicate worldwide by linking stations to track the spaceship and relay information to IBM computers in Washington, DC; Cape Canaveral; and Bermuda.

The computers controlling the *Friendship* 7 flight had been programmed with an incalculable number of equations that would control the capsule's trajectory from the time it lifted off at Cape Canaveral until it splashed down. It would land not far from Bermuda, where the navy would then retrieve it.

Glenn's safety was always paramount. He would not fly until we were as certain as we could be that he would be safe.

I was aware that John Glenn knew of my work. What I did not know at that time was that as he ran through his preflight checklist two days before the scheduled launch date, he was evaluating the data that the IBM computer had generated.

"Get the girl," he said, uncertain of the data from the computer. "If she says they're good, then I'm ready to go."

By "girl" he meant me, Katherine Johnson—Negro woman, widow, wife, sister, daughter, mother of three. Human computer.

In other words, he wanted me to calculate by hand the same numbers that had been fed into the electronic computer, to see if the answers I generated would match the computer's. If so, he'd have confidence that the machine had calculated his trajectory correctly.

I was sitting at my desk when one of the engineers picked up the phone and was amazed to receive that call. The very first time he traveled into the atmosphere and put his life on the line, one of our nation's heroes, astronaut John Glenn, knew that he could count on me.

This was an enormous assignment, and I felt its weight upon my shoulders. Then again, it was simply math—and math was my strong point.

Countless stacks of computer data sheets about the size and thickness of a DVD player were piled on top of my desk, and I recalculated the math for the entire trajectory of the voyage. It was a monumental task, but one I'd been preparing for since college. I was up to the challenge. I came up with answers for eleven different variables and calculated each one carefully.

It took me a day and a half to complete my computations.

To be especially safe, I took my calculations two decimal points beyond what the computer had come up with. The computer's results were, in fact, correct.

On the morning of February 20, 1962, people all around the United States gathered in front of their televisions to watch history in the making. In Florida, people traveled to Cape Canaveral itself and lined both its beaches gleaming with sand and its asphalt-topped roadways, trying to catch a glimpse of the spaceship. Elsewhere, people crowded around televisions just spellbound as John Glenn walked confidently to the launch pad, squeezed himself into the tiny capsule, and shook the hands of the men in white jumpsuits who closed the door to the capsule, sealing him in for takeoff.

There was no turning back.

Over the television, the viewing audience heard the sound of his heartbeat, which NASA was monitoring. *Lub-dub. Lub-dub. Lub-dub.* I noted that it seemed much calmer than mine, as I sat in the office of the Space Task Group.

John Glenn weighed only 186 pounds, but we needed one-quarter million pounds of rocket fuel with thrust equal to 3.5 million horsepower to lift him into space and get him safely home again.

We all had sweaty palms during the countdown, but the rockets fired perfectly at 9:47 a.m., and amid the fire and smoke as the rocket lifted off, Glenn was launched into the atmosphere!

Over the next four hours, fifty-five minutes, and

twenty-three seconds, he orbited the world three times, at more than seventeen thousand miles per hour.

But all was not well. During the first orbit, the automatic control system malfunctioned. After that Glenn was forced to operate the craft manually. During the second orbit, the heat shield came loose. My heart started pounding. If it came off, Glenn would be exposed to three-thousand-degree heat as he reentered Earth's atmosphere, about the same temperature as the sun. We had to prepare for the worst.

The whole world stood by breathlessly, wondering if he would be incinerated when he reentered Earth's atmosphere and the capsule emitted flames.

Despite some flames, thankfully nothing happened.

Glenn landed in the Atlantic Ocean near Grand Turk Island in the Bahamas. The capsule bounced in the waves for twenty-one minutes, until the navy destroyer *Noa* picked him up. We had sent a man into space, and John Glenn became an American hero.

Our next major mission was to land a man on the moon.

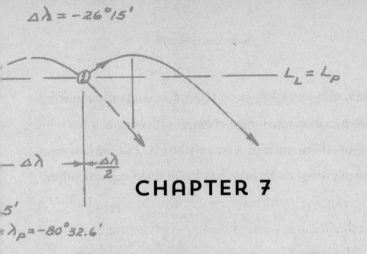

$\Delta\lambda = -26°15'$

$L_L = L_P$

$-\Delta\lambda$ $\dfrac{\Delta\lambda}{2}$

$5'$

$\lambda_P = -80°32.6'$

# CHAPTER 7

While we had focused our gaze upon the stars, a lot of cosmic change had been happening here on Earth.

Connie and Kathy had both started college—Connie at Hampton Institute and Kathy at Bennett College in Greensboro, North Carolina. As I reflected upon the fact that all three girls were in school, I realized that they were continuing an amazing legacy. For not only had Mamá and Daddy outsmarted segregation and oppression and sent all four of their children to college, but our daughters would be college educated as well. That was quite an accomplishment in an era when the average Negro had been able to attain only an eighth-grade education, and only about 5 percent had graduated from college. The odds had been long, yet somehow we had accomplished it. I knew Jimmie was looking down on us from heaven and feeling very proud.

Our Kathy, Joylette, and Connie, all grown up.

Having the girls in college made me very anxious, though. The sit-ins to desegregate restaurants and cafeterias that were now taking place across the South had originated in Greensboro. Students at Bennett and another Negro university in Greensboro, North Carolina A&T, were on the front lines. Though thousands of Negro students lived in that town, they weren't allowed to eat in the restaurants. A young man named Jesse Jackson was the head of the student government at A&T. He would later go on to become a minister, well-known civil rights leader, and presidential candidate.

Many of the sit-ins were nasty and violent. Angry Whites would call the student protesters every foul name they could think of; then they would spit on, humiliate, and physically intimidate them. Grown men and women would pour sugar, cream, ketchup, food, and hot coffee over students' heads; sometimes the White residents would drag the protesters off their lunch-counter stools and then kick and beat them bloody.

During the spring semester of 1963, Kathy got involved. Afraid both for her safety and that she'd never be able to find work if she were arrested, I begged her not to participate. She insisted.

"I will *not* go to jail," she promised me.

"But how can you guarantee that?"

"Because I won't break any laws."

"You don't have to break the law for the police to arrest you!"

Kathy couldn't control what the police would do; nor could she control what the White residents of Greensboro might do—and segregationists didn't spare women. In Mississippi, a woman my age named Fannie Lou Hamer had been fired from her job and forced out of her home just for registering to vote. Her efforts to help other Negroes vote would cause her to be arrested, beaten, and shot at. Stories like these were fairly common.

I was terrified. Then again, I also understood that Kathy was only doing what students of my generation had done to help end lynching. I remembered that our parents had warned us, too, about the dangers of getting involved. Maybe each generation takes risks that make their parents nervous. Perhaps that is how a society moves forward.

Led by icons of the civil rights movement like James Farmer, some of the students from the Congress of Racial Equality (CORE) at North Carolina A&T and their local student leader engaged in a series of protests that led to the city's restaurants and cafeterias being desegregated. The students at Bennett and A&T were instrumental to the sit-ins' success.

Later, Kathy would tell me that while she wasn't arrested, her roommate, Pat, was among those who were. Kathy had had to call Pat's parents, down in Houston, to give them the news. It was only after the president of Bennett College, Dr. Willa B. Player, went public about the students' arrests and the federal government stepped in that the students were released.

In the midst of this, Joylette had graduated from Hampton with a degree in mathematics in 1962—just a few months after John Glenn took flight. She married her college sweetheart, Lawrence Hylick, and then began her career at NASA as a mathematician. Kathy transferred to Hampton during the summer of 1963. I have to admit that having Joylette at NASA and Kathy at Hampton allowed me to breathe more easily. I suspect they felt safer too. That same summer Connie married a Hampton grad, John Boykin; they moved to New Jersey and eventually had three children. (She would return to Hampton in her late twenties, complete her degree in 1973, and become a teacher.)

During this same era, civil rights activists known as Freedom Riders had begun challenging the laws of segregation by riding buses through Southern states, passing through towns such as Birmingham and Montgomery, Alabama, where one group of riders was assaulted and their bus burned by mobs of angry Whites. One of the Freedom Riders, John Lewis, of Georgia, would eventually become a renowned congressman. Around the South, local authorities were turning police dogs and fire hoses on the young protesters who were pressing our nation for equal opportunity and freedom now.

In August of 1963, the March on Washington for Jobs and Freedom took place in front of the Lincoln Memorial on the National Mall in Washington, DC. Sitting in front of my black-and-white television, the girls and I felt goose bumps all over us as gospel singer Mahalia Jackson sang an old Negro spiritual, "I Been Buked and I Been Scorned," and we heard the words of what would come to be known as Dr. Martin Luther King Jr.'s "I Have a Dream" speech.

After the speech, the crowd erupted into applause, and I took in the sea of humanity of roughly 250,000 people, which looked like it stretched from the Lincoln Memorial, along the Reflecting Pool, all the way down to the Washington Monument. I wanted my girls to participate fully in our great nation. I wanted them to be safe. And I wanted them to be free.

But Negroes' triumphs seemed to walk hand in hand with tragedy. Just a few months later, on November 22, 1963—only two years after President Kennedy had set forth his vision of putting a man on the moon—Joylette called me at work, crying.

*"President Kennedy has been shot!"*

"WHAT?!"

All of the breath left my body as Joylette told me that President Kennedy had been killed by an assassin's bullet as he and his wife, Jackie, the First Lady, had been riding through Dallas in an open convertible. Already home sick from NASA on that day, and for the two days that followed, Joylette stayed glued to the news and called me with updates. Our nation and NASA grieved, for not only had our society's norms been shattered by an assassin, but to see our president cut down at such an early age, leaving his wife and young children behind, broke us all. I will never forget the sight of his toddler, John-John, saluting his father's casket. As I watched Mrs. Kennedy and her children, I thought of my own family's loss.

After President Kennedy's death, the vice president, Lyndon Baines Johnson, assumed President Kennedy's place.

On July 2 of the following year, President Johnson signed the Civil Rights Act of 1964, which made it illegal to discriminate against people based on race, color, religion, sex, or national origin in public places or at work. It also forbade the use of federal funds for anything that discriminated against anyone, and authorized the federal government to enforce the integration of schools and penalize schools that didn't comply. Finally, the act banned authorities from unequally applying the requirements that people had to meet in order to vote—one of the ways used to prevent Negroes from exercising their right to vote. The act helped to level the playing field a bit more. But big differences existed between what the law said and what actually happened in schools and workplaces. In some ways many things changed, but in others very little was different.

Throughout that summer of 1964—Freedom Summer is what the young people called it—voter registration campaigns to sign up Negro voters took place in Mississippi and other Southern states. Throughout the South and even in some parts of the North, White segregationists continued to terrorize our people, burning down homes, businesses, and churches, because the idea of Negroes being equal to Whites apparently scared them so much. I have always struggled to understand why.

We didn't know it then, but the civil rights movement was nearing its peak. Young people had begun embracing and feeling proud of Negro history and culture rather than running away from or being ashamed of it. Our girls allowed their hair to grow out naturally into styles called Afros. Young people began to call each other "Black" (and, later, "African American") instead of "Colored" or "Negro," and many younger folks began to grow tired of the incremental change that the older adults favored, and began pushing for more dramatic progress toward equality and "Black power."

As if this weren't enough going on, the Vietnam War was taking place and young men were being drafted. In fact, every Monday Jim would go to Hampton's campus to do physical training with the Reserve Officers' Training Corps (ROTC) cadets. As part of that training, they would run across campus together in formation. I always marveled at how, even in his midforties and into his fifties, Jim could keep up with young men half his age. He continued to work with the ROTC until well into his seventies.

Kathy's boyfriend, Donald Moore, an architecture major, was in the ROTC. He graduated in May of 1964 as a second lieutenant, and they got married at our home church, Carver Memorial, in July 1965. They went to Texas, where he was stationed, quite fortunately, as a teacher, rather than being sent off to war as so many young men were. (She would eventually complete her degree at Hampton in 1970 and become an educator.)

Women were actively fighting for their rights during that era too. Then led by Dr. Dorothy Height, the National Council of Negro Women focused on the economic problems facing Black women. The National Organization for Women was formed in 1966. The Black Panther Party for Self-Defense, which opposed police brutality and engaged in political and social programs in big cities, was founded that year too.

Just as all of these changes were taking place in American society, revolutionary things were happening within NASA as well.

A new idea had been developed for how to get to the moon, called lunar-orbit rendezvous. According to this concept you first needed to blast out of the atmosphere and stabilize a mother spacecraft inside of Earth's orbit. Then you would launch a smaller manned spacecraft from that mother ship, and the smaller craft would fly to the moon. Once on the moon, the astronauts would get out of that craft, called a Lunar Lander, in order to study the moon's surface. The Lunar Lander needed to be able to blast off from the moon and reconnect with the mother ship for the trip back to Earth. The process would require three astronauts. All three would take off from Earth together. One would stay in the mother ship, and the other two would travel from the mother ship in the Lunar Lander. Then they would all return to Earth together.

Each of these stages would need to be tested. Equally important, this concept required a spaceship so large—three hundred thousand pounds—that the nation's existing factories, railroads, highways, and ships wouldn't be able to transport the parts required to put it together. The US Army Corps of Engineers would need to think these things through and figure out how to make them happen.

We also had to know whether human beings could survive outside of their spacecraft. Weightless, would they drift away into the great beyond? Would their equipment work outside of the spaceship? These are some of the questions that NASA's scientists, engineers, mathematicians, and others were trying to figure out.

We knew there were huge gaps in our experience and knowledge, but we were determined to land a man on the moon—and to do so by the end of the decade as President Kennedy had promised.

Through all of our other efforts at space travel, we had been learning about things such as the Earth's magnetosphere—where the planet's magnetic field is stronger than the magnetic field of outer space—solar wind, and the Van Allen radiation belts, a collection of electrically charged particles around the Earth that protect our atmosphere from destruction. We had gained that knowledge in a series of small steps, each of which had built upon the other—all of which had been tremendously expensive.

With the backdrop of the civil rights movement and televisions that increasingly broadcast our nation's inequity and high rates of poverty, many people—including a lot of Negroes—started criticizing our work, calling it extravagant and insensitive to all the people who struggled just to get by here on Earth. Having come from very modest circumstances myself, I could definitely understand their point. In the face of this criticism, NASA began to try to make our work more relevant to the average citizen.

All along, amazing breakthroughs had been taking place as a result of space science. These improvements bettered the quality of everything ranging from radios, to television sets, to small electronic calculators, yet the agency hadn't done a good job of explaining these benefits to the public. For example, communications satellites allowed events like the Olympics to be covered in real time from any place in the world; airlines could offer reservation systems that would help people travel from coast to coast; banks could now have nationwide networks that would allow them to transmit information between locations. Weather satellites allowed scientists to spot, monitor, and track hurricanes before they made landfall, saving lives and protecting property. In medicine, a new generation of pacemaker could regulate a person's heartbeat for decades, rather than needing to be replaced every two years. Solar cells and nickel-cadmium batteries harnessed energy and created the promise of battery-powered cars. All of these breakthroughs and more had their roots in space science.

NASA also began to partner with universities, creating on-campus research programs and a greater demand for scientists, engineers, and people who studied what we now call the STEM disciplines—science, technology, engineering, and math. The need for them grew, well . . . astronomically, as did STEM educational opportunities.

These advances didn't solve our nation's inequality, but they did prove that our work was relevant and beneficial to society at large.

* · * · * * · * · * * · * * · *

Over the course of the decade, a series of space missions confirmed that the idea of having a launch vehicle that separated from the mother ship would, in fact, work. Several more missions tested the idea of spacecraft that could rendezvous and dock to each other. Still others tested whether astronauts would be able to work outside of their spacecraft. On one mission, the astronaut had so much fun floating around outside of the space capsule that his commanders had to order him to go back inside his craft. In general, though, we learned that, as thrilling as it looked, trying to maneuver a body suddenly weightless out in space could actually be quite tiring for the person.

In 1964, we received great medical news—that the slower heartbeat, loss of calcium in bones, pooling of blood in the legs, and other effects of weightlessness seemed to be temporary. The astronauts' bodies stabilized after a few days back on Earth. All of these things were very positive. People could live in space—at least for a while.

Then on January 27, 1967, a space flight numbered AS-204, later known as *Apollo 1*, was moving through its preflight tests to send the first manned space flight to the moon. Astronauts Virgil I. Grissom, Edward H. White II, and Roger B. Chaffee were sitting in the command module as the command center counted them down toward a launch. The countdown had reached T minus ten minutes.

To this day no one quite understands what happened next.

One of the astronauts reported that the spacecraft was on fire. Then the guys on the ground crew on the launch pad saw a flash fire break through the craft's shell, which was quickly swallowed in smoke. For five torturous minutes, the crew tried to open the hatch and get the astronauts out. But the fire quickly consumed all the oxygen, and our boys suffocated. How could they have been so close yet still die? Later, we'd learn that there had been a short circuit somewhere among the hundreds of miles of wiring within the craft. Exactly where, nobody knew. Not only did these courageous men lose their lives, but families lost their sons, wives lost their husbands, and children lost their fathers. Though our family tragedy had been different, Joylette, Connie, Kathy, and I knew how loss felt. The nation was shattered. Everyone grieved.

When things go wrong, you have to figure out what happened—whether it's people, the process, the mechanical systems, electrical systems. You figure it out and make changes no matter how painful those changes are.

The investigation discovered that the basic design of the spacecraft was sound, but there had been mistakes in design and in testing procedures. Later that year, US Air Force Major Robert Lawrence Jr., a physical chemist and the first Negro selected to become an astronaut, was killed when a supersonic jet he was in crashed at Edwards Air Force Base in California. Because the program he was working on was classified, few Americans ever knew what had happened.

We could not afford to fail again. NASA employees and all our partners and suppliers vowed to work closely to do an even better job.

Back home, Jim and I would often watch TV together as we tried to make sense out of what was happening in Negro society.

On February 21, 1965, Malcolm X, a civil rights activist and a former leader of the Nation of Islam, an organization of Negro American Muslims, was assassinated in New York. Less than one month later, on March 7, 1965, Bloody Sunday took place as a group of about six hundred peaceful protesters, almost all of them Negroes, led by Martin Luther King Jr., attempted to cross the Edmund Pettus Bridge leaving Selma on a march to Montgomery, located fifty-four miles away. They were beaten with whips and nightsticks by tear-gas-wielding White Alabama police officers. Night after night the violence and brutality against peaceful people throughout the South and beyond, who were protesting for basic rights, were broadcast on television for the entire world to see, shocking the nation and calling into question our country's claim to be the leader of the free world.

On August 6 of that year, President Johnson signed the Voting Rights Act of 1965, prohibiting the literacy tests that for decades had been used to keep Negroes from voting, primarily in the South. Negroes had found ourselves in a circular loop: We couldn't get a good education because our schools were inferior, and we were discriminated against at work. But when so many of us showed up to vote to try to change those situations, we were disqualified if we couldn't read well. The Voting Rights Act also allowed federal observers to review voter qualifications and monitor polling places.

We were slowly making progress, but then a breathtaking tragedy took place. Dr. Martin Luther King Jr. was assassinated on the evening of April 4, 1968, at the Lorraine Motel in Memphis, Tennessee, where he'd been organizing the city's sanitation workers to help them fight against poor working conditions and unequal pay. The news of Dr. King's death brought us all to our knees.

If he, who had advocated nonviolence rather than nationalism or separatism had been killed, what hope did the rest of us Negroes have? What chance remained that our children might see racial equality within our lifetimes? The thought that racial segregation and inequality might continue forever made it difficult for us to breathe. I mourned for his wife, Coretta, and his four children.

Kathy was on campus at Hampton, where the bells of the chapel started ringing. The students gathered around the shared televisions in their dorms, crying and trying to comfort one another. She called Jim and me many times, trying to figure out what was going to happen next and whether they were safe.

That evening the Negroes in Hampton stayed in the cocoon of our segregated neighborhoods, gravitating to our churches to try to make sense of our collective tragedy. Jim and I headed to Carver Memorial, where we cried together with our congregation, our pastor addressed us, members shared their memories and fears, and we sang church hymns and old Negro spirituals—the songs that had helped our ancestors survive.

That night protests broke out in Baltimore; Washington, DC; Newark; and other cities around the country. I worried that they might affect Joylette, who was now living with her husband in East Orange, New Jersey, with my first grand-children, Laurie and Troy. The state of Virginia would not hire her accountant husband, Lawrence, because he was a Negro. East Orange was located near Newark, where riots had taken place the previous summer to protest inequality and the lack of opportunity for the city's Negro residents. We spoke by phone many times over the following days. Jim and I prayed that Joylette, Lawrence, and the children would stay safe.

What was happening to our nation? Negroes pushed forward and made progress, increasingly advocating for Black power, which encouraged racial pride and pushed for more dramatic action to achieve equality, rather than just the incremental change toward equality that many Negro leaders espoused. Shirley Chisholm became the first Negro woman elected to Congress. As we slowly gained some civil rights, it seemed that both hope and calamity walked hand in hand.

As all of these things were going on throughout society, at NASA we were drawing closer to actually sending men to the moon. My role was to help calculate the trajectory of the Lunar Lander that would get them there. We needed to know where and when the rocket had to be launched in order to put it on the right trajectory.

The calculations were very challenging. For example, I had to consider the rotation of the Earth. Equally important was the location of the moon—where it was when the astronauts took off and where it would be when they got there. You're going this way because you want to intersect with the moon's path, but the moon is going that way. Then we had to synchronize the Lunar Lander, called the *Eagle*, with the command and service module (which would continue to orbit the Earth), so that our guys could all come home. It was intricate, but it was possible.

Safety had always been key, but after the *Apollo 1* AS-204 disaster, we scrutinized our efforts to make sure that everything would be as safe as possible. We checked. We double-checked. We rechecked that. We looked at even the smallest issues and made sure that we accounted for them by assessing their risk.

In the meantime the clock was ticking as we drew closer and closer to the end of the decade in which President Kennedy had promised we would put a man on the moon. Our men's safety was more important than the promise, but we felt confident we could do both.

On December 21, 1968, we got one important step closer, when *Apollo 8* lifted off into space. For the first time, three astronauts passed out of Earth's gravitational field and into that of the moon. The spacecraft had been fitted with a color TV camera, and all of the world could see the blue oceans, brown landmasses, and white clouds swirling around our planet against the pitch-black of outer space. For all of our differences down here on Earth, for the first time we were able to see a vision of humankind that didn't have any borders.

The men even flew around to the dark side of the moon, an anxiety-producing time when we lost radio contact with them, before they came back around and eventually returned to Earth.

Five months after that, *Apollo 10* took off and proved that the Lunar Lander could dock with the command module. Now every single step had been tested.

All systems were go!

The *Apollo 11* space flight took place on July 16, 1969. Astronauts Neil Armstrong, Edwin "Buzz" Aldrin, and Michael Collins were set to become the first human beings to land on the moon. By the time they actually blasted off, my calculations had long been completed and the now-reliable electronic computers—some programmed with my computations—had taken over. There would be no last-minute need for me to be called in as had happened with John Glenn. In fact, not only was I not at NASA during *Apollo 11*'s three-day trip to the moon, but I was in the Pocono Mountains in Pennsylvania, at a convention of my AKA sorority sisters, celebrating Black women's commitment to excellence.

On July 20, when Neil Armstrong said, "Houston, Tranquility Base here. The *Eagle* has landed," indicating that the Lunar Lander was actually on the moon, I was sitting on the floor, mesmerized by what I was watching on TV, just as the sorority sisters surrounding me were.

None of the women had any idea quite how nervous I was as I watched Armstrong.

When he stepped onto the moon and uttered those famous words, "That's one small step for a man, one giant leap for mankind"—a phrase heard by roughly 530 million people all around the world—none of my sorors, as I call them, was aware that I understood exactly what was taking place. Nor did any of them understand just how incredibly proud I was when Armstrong stuck an American flag into the surface of the moon, marking the fact that the United

States had not only put a man on the moon, but also that we had come from behind and beaten the Russians, and by doing so had won the Space Race.

Yet my calculations had not only helped the *Eagle* land successfully, but they also helped it to sync back up with the command and service module so that our guys could come back home.

The nation might still have thought of our people as inferior, but a Black woman had performed the computations that had taken White male astronauts into outer space, landed them on the moon, and brought them back safely to their families again. By then I was already working on calculations for a mission to Mars.

Until recently this story remained unpublished, hidden and overlooked just as were the stories of an incalculable number of figures in the history of Black people in the United States. But the truth be told, while amazing, mine is just one tale in a long and unending chain of Black heroism and excellence that began long ago and took place in countless families across multiple generations—and continues to this day.

At my retirement luncheon with NASA Assistant
Branch Head Ed Fondriot.

# EPILOGUE

**W**hen Astronauts Armstrong and Aldrin landed on the moon, I was excited to see so many people become intrigued by some of the same things I have been interested in for so long. I was also excited to receive an award for being on the Apollo team. One of my most prized possessions is a flag that flew to the moon and back.

I have to admit that I grew a little teary as I thought of my mother's attention to our schooling and my father's insistence that his children would go to college—even though they'd never met other Colored children who had benefited from that experience. I was excited to return home to White Sulphur Springs to be with all of our extended family—

including now six grandchildren: Laurie and Troy, but also Michele, Greg, Doug, and Michael—to celebrate Mamá and Daddy's fiftieth anniversary of marriage in the coming years.

I often think about Professors Evans and Claytor and all of my other teachers who not only saw my promise, but also helped me create a vision for my life that I'd never seen before—a vision that they'd never witnessed any Colored person experience either, but that I stepped into and that my children and grandchildren now walk in. During all my years at NASA, I never stopped tutoring, always remembering how powerful it can be to speak life into a young person's spirit and help expand the vision of what's possible for his or her future, especially as it involves math and science.

I love the stars, and it was a joy to contribute to the literature about space that was being published, but I had no idea that things would go this far—or that I or my accomplishments would become so well known.

The book *Hidden Figures*, written by Margot Lee Shetterly about the West computers, and the subsequent movie *Hidden Figures*, which was inspired by my life and the other women of West Computing, ended with Alan Shepard's trip into the atmosphere. Neither that nor putting a man on the moon was the end of my career, though. I worked at NASA for almost twenty-five more years. During this time I was involved with the Space Shuttle program, including its first launch in 1981 of the Space Shuttle *Columbia*, and the Earth Resources Satellite, which monitored clouds and atmospheric conditions over the oceans as well as land, including in remote places, allowing us to detect hurricanes, sandstorms, and ice conditions in both the northern and southern hemispheres.

I continued writing and publishing as well. I also reveled in some notable NASA firsts, including the first woman astronaut, Dr. Sally Ride—a physicist—and air force pilot and aerospace engineer Guion "Guy" Bluford, the first African American astronaut to make it to space. Both of these astronauts went into space in 1983. I prayed for the souls and families of physicist Dr. Ronald McNair, the second African American astronaut to go to space, and Christa McAuliffe, the first teacher to become an astronaut. They lost their lives when the Space Shuttle *Challenger* exploded in 1986. And I toasted

Dr. Mae Jemison, a chemical engineer and medical doctor, who became the first African American woman astronaut, in 1992.

Receiving an honorary degree from Capitol College in Maryland.

By the time I retired in 1986, after thirty-three years at Langley, I had authored or coauthored twenty-six research reports and tutored countless students.

Since my retirement, I have stayed busy.

Being involved in the *Hidden Figures* project was a joy. I or members of my family got to spend time with young women such as Taraji P. Henson, who portrayed me; Janelle Monáe, who played another of my coworkers, Mary Jackson; and Octavia Spencer, who played Dorothy Vaughan. They are thoughtful, intelligent, and really amazing young women. It is exciting to know that Black women are beginning to have these types of opportunities. I'd say the movie was about 75 percent accurate. The changes were to make it more enjoyable—for instance, I never ran across campus to use the bathroom. Believing that I was no better but no worse than anyone else—segregation or not—I used the bathroom closest to me. However, I was the exception to the rule.

Some things were way too complicated to explain in a two-hour movie. During most of the time when I was employed at NASA, I commuted to work with just one woman—fellow mathematician Eunice Smith (sadly, Alta Brooks passed away). Kirsten Dunst's character, Vivian Mitchell, was fictional, but she represented the attitudes and actions of some of the White women in management back then. Kevin Costner's character, Al Harrison, was based upon several people, including Robert R. Gilruth, who headed the Space Task Group. The character Paul Stafford, played by Jim Parsons, represented a number of the engineers I worked with, including Carl Huss, John Mayer, and Alton Mayo, as well as Ted Skopinski and Al Hamer, both of whom I was published with.

The film has unleashed a flurry of activity, which has been exciting to experience so late in my life, when so many of my contemporaries have either passed on or been forgotten about. I have to admit that I don't always understand all the fuss, though. I was just doing the job that I loved and had dreamed of.

One of my greatest honors occurred in 2015 when I was ninety-seven years old. That's when I was invited to the White House to meet our nation's first African American leader, President Barack Obama, and our First Lady, Mrs. Michelle Obama. Oh my, that was such a privilege! But I have a funny story to tell you. It took a lot of work to get past the Secret Service!

We were in the hotel room, reading all of the requirements before heading over.

"Oh shoot! I didn't bring Mama's photo ID," Kathy said.

So the adventure began.

"You don't have *anything*?" the security officer asked when we arrived at the White House and Kathy told him of our plight.

"Nope," Kathy said. "Nothing."

"We faxed it to you several days ago," Joylette informed the officer. "We didn't know that we'd need it again."

"Well, ma'am, do you know your Social Security number?" the officer asked me.

"I'm ninety-seven years old; I don't remember those numbers," I told him.

"Well, do you know your date of birth?"

That question I knew the answer to, of course, so they let me in. One way or another, they would have let me in anyway—I think!

That day, President Obama awarded me the highest honor our nation can award a civilian: the Presidential Medal of Freedom. It was a wonderful experience, one that I'll cherish for the rest of my life.

I've even been told that Reverend Eder, the White priest whose clothing my mother used to wash back in White Sulphur Springs, bought a sort of commemorative brick and had it installed in the wall at the National Cathedral in Washington, DC, in honor of my father, Joshua Coleman.

In 2017, when I was ninety-nine, something wonderful happened that I must admit I think is just a little crazy. NASA opened a 37,000-square-foot building named in my honor: the Katherine G. Johnson Computational Research Facility. Now, here's what's so surprising about that. During all the time I worked at NASA, I never looked for any personal credit—I was always a member of a team. Yet now there's this huge building named after me. Oh well. I guess life can be unexpected at times. I'm very proud of what NASA is doing today and why.

I've received lots of awards during my lifetime. But some

At the ribbon cutting ceremony for the research center named in my honor.

With my grandson, Troy Hylick (back right) and his math students at East Camden Middle School in New Jersey.

of the most meaningful and rewarding conversations I have are with schoolchildren. I have received so many letters over the years from students writing to thank me for my achievements and for allowing them to see someone who looks like them—whether a girl or a person of color—in a career that requires scientific, technological, engineering, or mathematical know-how.

One girl who was working on a project about me called me long-distance. We had been talking for a while when she said, "Are you still alive?"

"Yes, I'm alive," I told her. "I'm talking to you."

"But your picture is in the textbook. You're supposed to be dead!"

"Well, one day I'll be dead," I told her. "But don't give up on me yet!"

Sometimes people will ask me, "What good does it do us to go to space?" In return I often ask them, "Well, what good does it do you to stay home?"

Space is out there. We want to know all about it and we are able to go there. Why not learn what you can about it and get involved?

Jim and I set sail.

# ACKNOWLEDGMENTS

Thank you so much to my parents, Joshua and Joylette, and to Jim, my husband of fifty-nine years, and to my wonderful daughters, Joylette and Kathy, and to the memory of my free-spirited daughter Connie. You have been the light of my life and the joy of my existence. I cannot tell you how much I appreciate your assistance in getting my story out so that it can inspire the next generation of young people to *always* do their very best.

My deepest thanks to Hilary Beard for her research and hard work; Donyale Reavis, for her great legal counsel; and Jennifer Lyons, our literary agent. I am grateful as well to my editor, Reka Simonsen, and the team at Atheneum Books, including Julia McCarthy, Clare McGlade, Greg Stadnyk, Karyn Lee, Lisa Moraleda, Milena Giunco, and Justin Chanda.

# REACHING
## *for the*
# MOON

By Katherine Johnson

**1.** Katherine thinks often of her father's words: "You are no better than anyone else, but nobody else is better than you." Why are these words of wisdom so important to her? When in her life does she apply them, and how does it work out?

**2.** Growing up, Katherine repeated an adage in her Black community: "You have to be twice as good in order to be thought of as half as good." Note examples of this from Katherine's own experiences. Compare the qualifications of the Black "computers" at NASA to those of the White "computers." Why do you think the White women needed fewer credentials? What do you think about the adage and this assessment?

**3.** Katherine draws an admiring portrait of her parents. What makes them important to her? What are their goals for their children, and do the children reach those goals? Give examples of how her parents sacrificed for their children's futures. How might Katherine's life have turned out differently if she didn't have her parents' expectations, encouragement, and support?

**4.** Discuss the role of education in Katherine's life and success. Where does she go to school? What kind of student is she? In what ways does she surprise her teachers? How does she give back to her community through education?

**5.** Name some of Katherine's important teachers and mentors, and explain how they help her. Where does she meet them, and why do they encourage her? In contrast, who are the people she encounters who try to keep her from succeeding? What lessons do you think Katherine learns when facing those who don't believe in her?

**6.** Why did Whites deny Blacks access to education for so long? What were some of the dangers that enslaved people faced when learning to read? What were other ways that Whites made it hard for Blacks to get an education, both before and after the Civil War?

**7.** Katherine makes it clear that life can be dangerous due to racial hatred. "Mobs and even communities of angry Whites used terror to enforce the norms of segregation," she writes. Find and discuss examples of terrorism perpetrated by the Klan and others in her life and times. How does it affect Katherine and her community? Think about everyday interactions and comments, intentional or unintentional, that perpetuate prejudices and stereotypes; these are known as microaggressions. Can you find examples of those situations in the book, and Katherine's reactions to them?

**8.** "I loved numbers and numbers loved me," Katherine writes early on in her autobiography. What do you think she means by that? Why does she love numbers so much? In what way do they love her? How does her love of numbers help her to succeed in life?

**9.** In discussing numbers, Katherine's father says to her brother, Charles, "Once you understand the background of any idea, you can figure any problem out for yourself." What does he mean by that? How does Katherine apply that advice to mathematics and other problems that she encounters? How does the idea help her to teach math?

**10.** When Katherine first submits her application to NACA, later NASA, she has the feeling that the White woman who takes it might not pass it on. Nevertheless, she doesn't give up. "Having patience was part of Negro life," she explains. How else might her experiences growing up in a segregated community have impacted the way she handles situations? Give examples from the book.

**11.** Describe Katherine's time at NASA as portrayed in the book. What was her role in the space program? What are some of her contributions? What resistance did she face? How did she feel about her work there?

**12.** In chapter five, Katherine describes a situation in which she finds a mistake in a White male engineer's math calculations. Why does she think pointing out the mistake might cause her trouble? "I'd crossed a social line, and everyone froze. I could almost hear some of the engineers thinking, *Who is she, a Colored woman, to question a White male engineer?*" Discuss her description of the incident and explain the outcome. Why do you think the engineers reacted that way?

**13.** Katherine married twice: her first marriage was to Jimmie Goble, who died in 1956, and her second is to Jim Johnson. How does she meet each man? What role do they each play in her life? Do they support Katherine's career? Describe the men's personalities as conveyed by the autobiography.

**14.** After her first husband dies, Katherine writes, "Bad things happen, and then life goes on." Do you think this is a good philosophy to follow? Explain your answer. Discuss her husband's death and how she copes with it. Give other examples of bad things that happen in her life before and after his death, and how she deals with them. Do you think any of these bad things change the way she views the world?

**15.** Discuss some of the personal characteristics that make Katherine so successful in her field, citing specific examples. Compare and contrast these with the traits that help Katherine face difficulties in her personal life as well as the hardships of life as a black woman.

**16.** Katherine notes that words used to describe race, such as African American, have changed over the years. Why do you think that is? Talk about the different words she uses throughout the book, and which ones are no longer considered acceptable. Why do you think she uses an initial capital letter for *White* as well as *Black* and *Colored*?

*Guide written by Kathleen Odean, a youth librarian for seventeen years, who chaired the 2002 Newbery Award Committee.*

*This guide has been provided by Simon & Schuster for classroom, library, and reading group use. It may be reproduced in its entirety or excerpted for these purposes.*

Looking for another great book?
Find it
**IN THE MIDDLE.**

Fun, fantastic books for kids
in the in-be**TWEEN** age.

IntheMiddleBooks.com

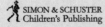

*Each time we fly back to our everyday
lives, one of my two selves
is left behind. . . .*

IN THIS HAUNTINGLY BEAUTIFUL MEMOIR,
Newbery Honor–winner Margarita Engle tells of
growing up with two cultures during a time of cold
hostility between the United States and Cuba, and
of the childhood that shaped this sensitive young
girl into an award-winning poet.

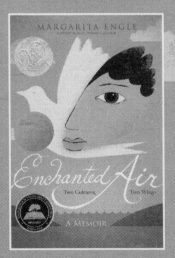

"This is a book to return to, page after
page, line after line. Exquisite."
—Kathi Appelt, author of Newbery
Honor and National Book Award finalist
*The Underneath*

★ "Beautifully told."
—*Kirkus Reviews,* starred review

★ "[A] worthy addition to any collection."
—*Booklist*, starred review

Atheneum

PRINT AND EBOOK EDITIONS AVAILABLE
simonandschuster.com/teen

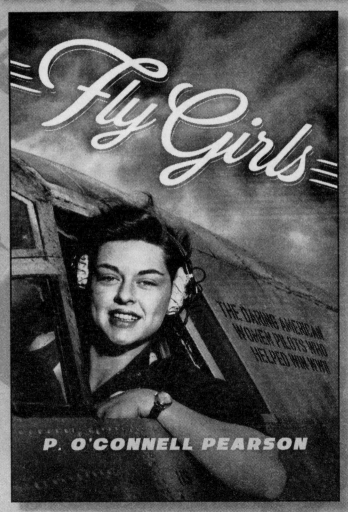